Also by Richard Nixon

SIX CRISES (1962)

RN: THE MEMOIRS OF RICHARD NIXON (1978)

THE REAL WAR (1980)

LEADERS (1982)

REAL
PEACE

REAL PEACE

by Richard Nixon

LITTLE, BROWN AND COMPANY · BOSTON · TORONTO

FIRST TRADE EDITION

First published in a privately printed edition in September 1983

LIBRARY OF CONGRESS CATALOGING IN PUBLICATION DATA

Nixon, Richard M. (Richard Milhous), 1913–
    Real peace.

    1. Peace.   2. International relations.   3. United
States—Foreign relations—Soviet Union.   4. Soviet
Union—Foreign relations—United States.   I. Title.
JX1963.N66   1983   327'.09'048   83-62597
ISBN 0-316-61149-2

MV

Published simultaneously in Canada
by Little, Brown & Company (Canada) Limited

PRINTED IN THE UNITED STATES OF AMERICA

*To the
peacemakers*

CONTENTS

The Myths of Peace   1

The Keys to Real Peace   15

NATO and Japan   55

China   68

The Third World   73

Peaceful Competition   95

REAL
PEACE

THE MYTHS OF PEACE

There can be no real peace in the world unless a new relationship is established between the United States and the Soviet Union.

The two superpowers cannot afford to go to war against each other, at any time or under any circumstances. Each side's vast military power makes war obsolete as an instrument of national policy. The cost to both sides of a full-scale conventional or nuclear war would far exceed any conceivable benefits.

In the nineteenth century the German military strategist Clausewitz called war "the continuation of political activity by other means." At that time national leaders used war or the threat of war as a last resort to extract concessions from their adversaries.

Now, for the superpowers, using that last resort would be suicide. In the age of nuclear warfare to continue our political differences by means of war would be to discontinue civilization as we know it.

1

War is an option whose time has passed. Peace is the only option for the future. At present we occupy a treacherous no-man's-land between peace and war, a time of growing fear that our military might has expanded beyond our capacity to control it and our political differences widened beyond our ability to bridge them.

The situation is precarious, but the moment is precious. It is imperative that the leaders of the United States and the Soviet Union seize the moment to achieve a major breakthrough for peace—not a mythical perfect peace but a real peace, based on a joint recognition of the harsh reality that they have profound, irreconcilable differences but that their survival depends on their finding ways to manage their differences without war.

A world war, whether conventional or nuclear, must never again be allowed to take place. One of the most empty-headed and dangerous fallacies of the nuclear disarmament movement is that the world would necessarily be better off without nuclear weapons. Those who survived the trench warfare of World War I, the Allied firebombings in Germany and Japan during World War II, or the Soviets' recent use of chemical warfare in Laos can testify that conventional war brings its own unique horrors.

We must not allow our understandable fear of a nuclear war to blind us to the increasingly awesome destructiveness of conventional weapons. Conventional weapons killed 15 million in World War I and over 54 million in World War II. Casualties in a conventional World War III would be far greater. We must face up to the fact that in any conventional or nuclear world war there will be no winners, only losers. Charles de Gaulle recognized this when he observed during our meeting at Versailles in 1969, "In the Second World War, all the nations of Europe lost; two were defeated."

The United States' superiority in nuclear weapons, which we no longer have, was the indispensable factor in deterring the Soviet Union from launching a conventional war against Western Europe after World War II. While war has become obsolete as an instrument of policy the tools of war must continue to play a role in keeping the peace. Military deterrence, including nuclear forces, is an essential component of any lasting peace. When each side holds an equally good hand, a potential aggressor is likely to keep both his hands on the table.

Paradoxically, though war is obsolete we live in a world that is perpetually at war. In this summer of 1983, fifteen wars and a score of minor conflicts are raging around the globe. Since World War II there have been 140 wars, resulting in the deaths of over ten million people. Many of these have been local conflicts in the Third World in which nations have fought over religion or territory, or in which people have risen up against unpopular leaders. But virtually all of them have been haunted by the specter of superpower confrontation.

In some cases the Soviet Union has initiated or exacerbated such conflicts; in other cases the U.S. has stepped in to protect its interests against communist aggression. As long as the superpowers view their interests and responsibilities on a global level, each small war is a world war in the making. Any guerrilla, no matter how obscure his cause or how remote his country, can fire a shot that will be heard around the world. A real peace between the superpowers must therefore take into account all conflict, everywhere in the world, and also those political, social, and economic tensions that lead to conflict.

Real peace will not come from some magic formula that will suddenly and once and for all be "discovered," like the promised land or the holy grail. Real peace is a process—a continuing process for managing and containing conflict between competing nations, competing systems, and competing international ambitions. Peace is not an end to conflict but rather a means of living with conflict, and once established it requires constant attention or it will not survive.

Confusing real peace with perfect peace is a dangerous but common fallacy. Idealists long for a world without conflict, a world that never was and never will be, where all differences between nations have been overcome, all ambitions forsworn, all aggressive or selfish impulses transformed into acts of individual and national beneficence.

Because of the realities of human nature, perfect peace is achieved in two places only: in the grave and at the typewriter. Perfect peace flourishes—in print. It is the stuff of poetry and high-minded newspaper editorials, molded out of pretty thoughts and pretty words. Real peace, on the other hand, will be the down-to-earth product of the real world, manufactured by realistic, calculating leaders whose sense of their nations' self-interest is diamond-hard and unflinching.

Those who make peace at the typing table rather than at the negotiating table have the luxury of being peacemakers without having to grapple with complex problems in the rough-and-tumble world of real international diplomacy. To them the only obstacle to peace is the regrettable lack of leaders who are as selfless and idealistic as they claim to be and who are willing to put aside parochial national interest in the interest of bringing peace to the world. They hope that this era will be the one in which self-interest, the force that has driven history since the dawn of history, will simply evaporate.

Perfect peace has no historical antecedents and therefore no practical meaning in a world in which conflict among men is persistent and pervasive. If real peace is to exist, it must exist along with men's ambitions, their pride, and their hatreds. A peace that fails to take these things into account will not last.

We will meet the challenge of real peace only by keeping in mind two fundamental truths.

First, conflict is a natural state of affairs in the world. Some nations are certain to be unsatisfied by what they have and will try to get more, for a variety of reasons and through a variety of means. Other nations will resist the designs of these acquisitive powers. One way or another nations in such positions will come into conflict, and if they cannot resolve their conflicts peaceably they will eventually try to resolve them violently.

Second, nations only resort to aggression when they believe they will profit from it. Conversely, they will shrink from aggression if it appears in the long run it will cost them more than it benefits them.

Short of changing human nature, therefore, the only way to achieve a practical, liveable peace in a world of competing nations is to take the profit out of war.

Most of the obstacles to peace today result from the Soviet Union's expansionist policies. But there are also those in the West who impede the peacemakers. A few, their allegiances and their motives clear, do so intentionally. Those who do so inadvertently are far more dangerous.

Lenin was fully aware of how helpful naive Westerners could be to the communist cause. He contemptuously called them "the useful idiots." More out of ignorance than by design, the useful idiots earnestly plug ridiculously simplistic answers to our most complex problems. They are the sloganeers whose idea of thoughtful analysis is often limited to what will fit on a t-shirt or a bumper sticker. "Make love, not war." "You can't hug your kids with nuclear arms." "Honk if you want peace." Much of this fatuous nonsense is harmless, but unfortunately not all the useful idiots occupy themselves by marching and honking for peace. Some teach in our universities; some write newspaper columns; others pontificate on television.

The complexities of the modern world are so baffling to them that they seek comfort in simple answers. What they fail to recognize is that for every complicated problem there is *always* a simple answer—and it's usually wrong.

Building a real peace will be arduous, frustrating work, and it is not surprising that some fall for shortcuts that promise to get them what they want quickly, painlessly, and cheaply. These shortcuts never work, and we should not expect them to work.

In his heart everyone knows that the only people who get rich from the "get rich quick" books are those who write them. But just as there are countless "get rich quick" schemes there is also a wide array of seductively appealing "get peace quick" schemes.

These are the myths of peace. Myths are fairy tales that people make up about things they otherwise would not understand. The ancients devised them to "explain" lightning and the changing of the seasons; today many concoct them to "explain" international relations. They are profoundly reassuring to those who otherwise would be profoundly confused by the complex dilemmas we face. But these myths are doubly dangerous: dangerous because they can distract and confound our leaders and clog decision-making channels, and also because of the chance that one of them might actually become official policy.

The Disarmament Myth. This is the granddaddy of peace myths, a favorite of generation after generation of idealists. Founded on a logical fallacy in which human intentions are equated with the means men use to carry out their intentions, the idea of disarmament has alternately seduced and disappointed peacemakers throughout history.

"Disarmists," those alarmists who think the world's greatest evil is the arms race, believe that it is the *existence* of arms that causes war rather than the political tensions which lead to their use. Because of this fundamental misconception, the disarmists' best hope for peace is a prescription for international disaster.

If we are to make any progress toward real peace we must accept the fact that war results from unresolved political differences, not from the existence of arms. Pursuing arms control talks without dealing with our other nation-to-nation problems at the same time would be the ultimate example of treating a symptom while letting the disease run its brutal course. It is like a doctor prescribing aspirin rather than penicillin as a cure for pneumonia.

One of the few arms control pacts of the twentieth century was concluded in 1922 at the Washington Naval Conference. The U.S., Britain, and Japan agreed to limit their naval forces by adopting a battleship ratio of 5-5-3; Japan had also signed a treaty with eight other powers agreeing to observe the integrity of China. But Japan's ambitions in the Far East and its resentment of the Western powers were both far greater than its commitment to the agreements it had signed. In 1931 it invaded China, and in 1941 it struck our naval forces at Pearl Harbor.

World War II resulted not from arms buildups but from the territorial ambitions of Japan and Germany. Germany's and Japan's arms buildups were a result of these ambitions, not the cause of them. The current arms race is between a similarly ambitious Soviet Union and a free world that has determined not to be caught off-guard again. The root causes of that conflict must be addressed before arms control can have any purpose.

The one sure way to prevent a nuclear holocaust would be to eliminate all nuclear weapons. But complete nuclear disarmament is an impossible dream. The reason is simple: nuclear weapons are simple. The principles of physics that make them possible are widely understood by governments, by terrorists, even by college undergraduates. The materials for making them are within the grasp of virtually every modern nation.

Some, out of desperation or supreme naivete, have suggested that an international authority be established to banish nuclear weapons and make sure they are never built again. Because such an authority would by necessity be privy to the inner workings of every government in the world, it would itself be the most powerful and ultimately the most dangerous institution on earth. Incredible political force would have to be brought to bear to keep nuclear weapons from being built, and that force would be so vast as to change the character of life on earth. Like the seventeenth-century political philosopher Thomas Hobbes, the disarmists are in effect asserting that we must offer ourselves and our liberties up to some superstate so that it can protect us from being devoured by each other in the nuclear state of nature.

That the disarmists would propose some outlandish "world government" shows that most of them, to put the most charitable light on the matter, are living in a dream world in which problems between nations can be solved by some authority other than national governments. This delusion is a form of radiation sickness. If you look directly at an atomic blast you may go blind; apparently intellectual blindness can result from contemplating the nuclear weapons issue for too long. Nuclear weapons will always exist. We must learn to live with what we know rather than wasting our energies in the pretense of not knowing it. But while we cannot eliminate nuclear weapons, we can do a great deal to prevent them from being used. It is only by learning to live in peace with our adversaries that we will learn to live with nuclear weapons.

The World Government Myth. After the cataclysm of World War II, in which 55 million people died, those who had served and survived returned home to the happy news of the United Nations conference in San Francisco. Everyone was hopeful that through this new organization we would debate about our disagreements rather than fight about them.

But as was the case with the League of Nations after World War I, the promise of the UN was illusory. The League of Nations and the UN were both noble but unavailing attempts to turn man's most idealistic impulses about peace into reality. Envisioned as the peacekeeper of the postwar world, the UN has been unable in most cases either to forestall war or to end a war once it was begun. One expert has concluded that of 93 separate conflicts between 1946 and 1977, the UN held limited debate on 40, did not debate at all about 53, and did not significantly contribute to the resolution of any.

Many nations are ably represented in the UN by dedicated, highly intelligent delegates, and the organization as a whole does important work in such areas as health and hunger relief. At its best the United Nations serves as a forum for the views and complaints of smaller nations that otherwise might be ignored in a world dominated by the superpowers. But at its worst it is more often than not a propaganda arm of the Soviet Union and its satellites and shills, a hall of distorting mirrors where peace-loving Russian armies are "invited in" by their victims, where the aiding and abetting of terrorism is actually "supporting wars of national liberation"—where, as in the world of George Orwell's *1984*, "war is peace" and "freedom is slavery." The UN has exacerbated many conflicts either by cavalierly blaming the U.S. or by ignoring the involvement of the Soviet Union. While 160 flags fly at the UN, the one that flies the highest is the double standard.

No major power will submit an issue affecting its basic interests to a forum in which it can be overruled by smaller powers. The UN's failure shows that international problems must be solved by negotiations between autonomous governments—or they will not be solved.

The Myth of Peace Through Trade. Optimism, like hope, springs eternal, and from each generation of leaders spring the eternal optimists who say that trade between aggressive adversaries softens their belligerence. Five years after the Russian Revolution David Lloyd George, the British prime minister, said that trade with the Soviets would "bring an end to the ferocity, the rapine, and the crudity of Bolshevism surer than any other method." Many in the West, eager for what they called "peaceful coexistence" with the new communist government, agreed. Western businessmen scrambled for access to what they hoped would be rich new Soviet markets, and the Russians obligingly granted over 300 "concessions" to Western companies. Eventually all these manufacturing firms were expelled, but not before Soviet engineers had studied and copied Western industrial technology and methods and put them to work during Stalin's massive industrial buildup in the 1930s.

That first round of economic cooperation in the 1920s did not bring the West and the Soviets closer together. It did help turn the Soviet Union into a much stronger adversary. Yet today there are many, especially in the Western business community, who share Lloyd George's view. Their optimism, though commendable, is again based on faulty logic. Peace-through-trade did not work before, and it will not work now. As Konrad Adenauer told me in 1967 just before his death, "Trade is trade." Nations enter into trading relationships in the hope of making a profit, and any nation with aggressive ambitions can be expected to use its profits in the pursuit of those ambitions.

In both world wars nations that had traded with each other fought each other. Before World War II Japan had trade ties with the U.S. that had been painstakingly built up since the nineteenth century. Germany traded extensively with each of the countries it invaded.

In the end both nations' leaders found their grievances and territorial ambitions to be far stronger than their desire to remain at peace and engage in peaceful commerce with their neighbors. Believing that they could profit more from war than from peace, they went to war. Their choice proved that just as weapons are dangerous only insofar as they may be used to resolve political differences, commerce with an adversary contributes to peace only if it is part of a larger structure designed to reduce political differences. Otherwise, by trading with an aggressive, expansionist power you are fueling a fire that could eventually consume you.

The Myth of Peace Through Friendship. Some of the useful idiots put no faith in leaders. Others put far too much. The latter believe that if leaders would only meet and get to know one another, peace would follow as a matter of course. Since they think international conflict results primarily from misunderstanding and bad communication, they assume that friendships between nations and treaties and agreements designed to set the world right will inevitably result from friendships between national leaders.

This has never been the case, in our century or in any other. William Jennings Bryan, Woodrow Wilson's first secretary of state, believed war could be prevented if nations would agree to meet amicably to settle their disputes, and he signed treaties with 30 nations creating mechanisms for doing so. World War I followed fast on Bryan's heels. In the 1930s Imperial Japan's promise to observe the integrity of China did not prevent or delay its invasion of Manchuria. In World War II Nazi Germany invaded the Soviet Union in 1941, thus violating the two-year-old Hitler-Stalin nonaggression pact.

History is a pathetic junkyard of broken treaties. Yet naive idealists persist in believing that summits, state dinners, windy toasts, tearful bearhugs and *abrazos*, and solemn signing ceremonies are the very essence of diplomacy. They put great faith in good relations among leaders, and their hearts swell when they turn on the evening news and see two "former" adversaries grinning and tipping glasses at each other.

The media frequently mistake such atmospherics for real diplomatic progress because they only scan the surface of events, accumulating photographs of smiles and handshakes to print and copies of agreements to excerpt and summarize. Following such a meeting the diplomatic correspondents count up all the smiles, handshakes, and agreements, scrutinize the texts of the dinner toasts, study how pleased the officials are with themselves on the flight home, determine how many souvenirs the diplomats' wives bought, and then, relying on a journalistic calculus known only to themselves, pronounce the event a success or a failure. In the end they and their readers will probably learn little or nothing about what actually happened when the leaders sat down by themselves and tackled the substantive issues. In front of the cameras the leaders had been friends joined in the pursuit of peace, but behind closed doors they reverted to their real selves: aggressor, victim, cat, mouse, hawk, chicken, winner, loser.

Handshakes do not change national ambitions or interests. "Friendship treaties" do not necessarily express or create friendship. When two leaders sit down to talk, they do not turn into philanthropists. They do not give away anything without getting something in return which they value as much or more. Good personal relations do not ensure good state relations. All leaders, not just communist leaders, put their nations' interests above their personal likes and dislikes.

Leaders go to meetings with adversaries in pursuit of good press back home, in search of leverage to use in relations with other nations, or in the hope of exploiting the other side's weaknesses or irresolution and coming out ahead as a result. International relations are not like lunch at the club or a round of golf with friends. They are more like entering a snake pit where good intentions and good manners, adhered to slavishly in the face of your enemy's malevolence, are bound to be distinct hindrances. No leader should meet with an adversary unless he is fully aware of his own strengths and weaknesses and those of his opponent; unless he has something he wants to bargain for and something to bargain with; and unless he is prepared to be worked over by professionals.

Face-to-face meetings between leaders of hostile powers always have been and will continue to be useful for only two reasons. First, they help the leaders get each others' measure and as a result help them avoid potentially disastrous miscalculations later on. Second, they provide a setting for the exceedingly delicate, difficult process of making agreements the observance of which will serve both sides' interests simultaneously. Unless agreements are self-enforcing they will not last. It is a reflection of the great difficulty of meaningful negotiation between adversaries that such agreements, amid all of history's friendship treaties and nonaggression pacts, have been few and far between.

In the long term we can hope that religion will change the nature of man and reduce conflict. But history is not encouraging in this respect. The bloodiest wars in history have been religious wars. Men praying to the same God killed each other by the thousands in America's Civil War and by the millions in World War I and World War II. Unless men change, a real peace must be built on the assumption that the most we can do is to learn to live with our differences rather than dying over them.

THE KEYS TO REAL PEACE

The door to real peace must be unlocked. Two keys are required to open it. The United States has one; the Soviet Union has the other. Unless the superpowers adopt a new live-and-let-live relationship, the world will not see real peace in this century. If we fail to work toward that end, suicidal war is inevitable. If we succeed in reaching it, not only does world war become avoidable, but world peace becomes possible. Working against each other, the superpowers will enter a spiral of escalating differences that could lead to war. Working together, they can be an irresistible force for peace not only for themselves but for others as well.

Never has real peace been so necessary and yet so difficult to achieve. The stark truth is that the ideologies and the foreign policies of the superpowers are diametrically opposed. The struggle between the Soviet Union and the United States is between an avowedly and manifestly aggressive power and an avowedly and manifestly defensive one, between a totalitarian civilization and a

15

free one, between a state that is frightened by the idea of freedom and one that is founded on it.

The United States wants peace; the Soviet Union wants the world. Our foreign policy respects the freedom of other nations; theirs tries to destroy it. We are interested in peace as an end in itself; they are interested in it only if it serves their ends. The Soviets pursue those ends unscrupulously, by means short of all-out war. They lie, cheat, subvert governments, disrupt elections, subsidize terrorists, and wage wars by proxy. For the Soviets, peace is a continuation of war by other means.

Russians and Americans can be friends. But the governments of the Soviet Union and the United States can never be friends because their interests are irreconcilable. The peace we seek cannot be based on mutual friendship. It can only be grounded on mutual respect for each other's strength.

We will continue to have political differences that will drive us apart. We must also recognize, however, that the United States and the Soviet Union have two common interests that can draw us together. As the world's two greatest military powers, we both want to avoid a major war that neither of us would survive. As the world's two major economic powers—each with enormous resources and capable people—we can cooperate in ways that could benefit both of us immensely.

We must not delude ourselves into believing that the East-West struggle is the result of a giant misunderstanding that can be overcome if we sit down and talk it over. We can form Soviet-American friendship societies or tip vodka glasses with Kremlin leaders, but it will not lead to peace. That approach assumes the Soviets share with the West a "sincere" desire for peace. But as Ambassador Charles Bohlen told me in 1959, "Trying to determine whether the Soviet leaders are sincere about anything is a useless exercise." Pointing to a coffee table, he added, "They are pure materialists. You can no more describe them as being sincere than you could describe that table as being sincere."

If our differences are so intractable, is peace possible? Our differences make a perfect, ideal peace impossible, but our common interests make a pragmatic, real peace achievable. We are entering a new phase of the East-West struggle. In view of the verbal missiles rocketing between Washington and Moscow, we might conclude that the chances for peace are remote. But if we look beyond the rhetoric to the realities, we can be more optimistic. The table is set for a breakthrough toward real peace.

In working for peace, we must not pursue the unachievable at the expense of the attainable. Neither we nor the Soviets can compromise our basic values. Only if we recognize that we are not going to settle our differences can we avoid going to war over them. The most we can hope to achieve is an agreement establishing peaceful rules of engagement for our continuing conflict. If we cannot walk arm-in-arm down the road toward peace, we must try at least to walk side-by-side.

The enormous military strength and the aggressive policies of the Soviet Union lead many in the West to conclude that the prospects for peace are virtually nonexistent. Their concerns are justified, and I have addressed them in *The Real War*. But our analysis of the Soviet position cannot stop with their troop and weapons count. In designing our foreign policy, we must know not only our adversary's strengths, but also his weaknesses. We must not wallow in despair about Soviet might, for then we will fail to focus our attention on Soviet vulnerabilities.

No man knows the strengths and weaknesses of the Soviet Union better than Yuri Andropov. For fifteen years he was the head of the KGB, the Soviet espionage and police apparatus. There he received reports from the vast network of Soviet agents at home and abroad and travelled extensively throughout the Eastern bloc. We can be certain that as he steps up to bat, he knows the score, knows the other team, knows how to play the game, and is prepared to put more than pine tar on his bat.

The West knows little about Andropov himself. When he came into power, he was the subject of intense speculation in the West. Some media observers suggested that he was a closet liberal, a pussycat who would be easy to deal with because he liked American jazz and drank Scotch rather than vodka. Such commentators are forever confusing style with substance. They are suckers for style because style is their bread and butter. In the 1950s, they dismissed Nikita Khrushchev as a lightweight because he spoke bad Russian, drank too much, wore ill-fitting clothes, and had crude manners. They were wrong about Khrushchev, and they are wrong about Andropov. Anyone who claws his way to the top in the murderous jungle warfare of the Soviet hierarchy is bound to be a formidable adversary. Only the strong survive and reach the top in communist regimes.

We know this for sure about Andropov. He is an intelligent, dedicated, ruthless communist who shares the global ambitions of every Soviet dictator since the Bolshevik Revolution. Those who expect the Soviet Union to moderate its belligerence as soon as Andropov consolidates his power are deluding themselves.

Fortunately, however, he is a hard-headed pragmatist, not a madman. This makes him less dangerous in the short run but potentially more dangerous in the long run, unless we develop pragmatic policies that will affect his interests.

Andropov knows the strengths of the Soviet Union. He can point to some significant achievements over the past decade. Since 1974, over 100 million people have come under communist domination or have been lost to the West. Most ominously, the Soviets have gained superiority over the West in the most powerful and accurate nuclear weapons, land-based strategic and intermediate-range ballistic missiles.

Today the Soviets, through their Cuban and Nicaraguan surrogates, are threatening to make Central America the next East-West battleground. Through their Libyan proxies, they are advancing in Central Africa. They are inching, via Afghanistan, toward the Persian Gulf. Through their support of Syria and the radical Palestinians, they are trying to exacerbate the Arab-Israeli conflict. By supporting both Iran and Iraq they are positioning themselves to pick up the pieces after that war in the oil-rich Persian Gulf. Their propaganda machine is operating at full throttle, helping fuel the disarmament movement in Western Europe and thus continuing their 35-year-old campaign to divide the West against itself. The overall picture they present to the West is one of enormous power that backs up a menacing, expansionist foreign policy.

But Andropov is no fool. He is also aware of the profound weaknesses of the Soviet Union. Its economy is in desperate shape. Western economies have been through some rough seas, but the Soviet economy is dead in the water. The growth rate is plummeting. Productivity is dropping. Absenteeism, corruption, malingering, and drunkenness are rife. The standard of living is sinking, so much so that the life expectancy of Russian men is actually going down. The *average* wage of workers in the Soviet Union is lower than Brazil's *minimum* wage. Japan, with one-half the population of the Soviet Union, less arable land than California, no oil and very few natural resources, has a gross national product almost as large as that of the Soviet Union and a per capita income three times as high.

Andropov's vastly overblown military budget only increases the problem. It is twice as large as ours in terms of the proportion of GNP it consumes. That creates an enormous drag on the economy, reducing the incentives for individuals to produce goods and limiting potential future growth. After 60 years of big promises and poor performance, the stark truth is there for all to see. Soviet socialism does not work.

The ideology of communism has lost its appeal. Communists have never won a majority in a free election anywhere in the world. The crisis in Poland is only the most visible example of the popular discontent that is heating up just beneath the surface and threatens to boil over throughout Eastern Europe and in the Soviet Union itself. A scene I remember from my trip to Poland in 1959 illustrates this. Even now I can see the members of a crack Polish honor guard standing on a flatbed truck, cheering, and raising their hands in the "V-for-victory" sign as our motorcade left the Warsaw airport. The Kremlin's military planners are daydreaming if they are counting on the loyalty of Polish troops in the event of a war in Europe.

Never in history has an aggressive power been more successful in extending its domination over other nations and less successful in winning the approval of the people of those nations. As has been the case since the end of World War II, millions of refugees are on the move today. The traffic is all one way—from communism to freedom.

The costs of Soviet conquests are a massive drain on its desperately weak economy. The British may have been enriched by their empire, but the Soviets are being impoverished by theirs. Andropov must pour huge economic resources into his empire to keep his shaky political investments afloat. Cuba costs him $14 million a day. Angola, Ethiopia, Vietnam, and Nicaragua cost him over $5 million a day. Afghanistan has cost him millions of dollars and thousands of casualties. The resistance Soviet puppet regimes are meeting in Afghanistan, Angola, Mozambique, Ethiopia, and Nicaragua proves that the Soviet Union is increasingly unable to digest what it swallows.

On its Western front, the Soviet Union faces a newly united NATO. America's allies, without whom a comprehensive peace would be impossible, are acting with vision and strength under the leadership of conservatives like Margaret Thatcher and Helmut Kohl and anti-Soviet socialists like François Mitterrand and Bettino Craxi. The alliance is united behind a program to redress the European balance of power by deploying American Pershing II and cruise missiles. The Soviet propaganda campaign has failed. Andropov must now know that these deployments will begin by the end of the year unless he concludes an arms control agreement in Geneva.

On its Eastern front, the Soviet Union faces its greatest long-term challenge. Under the leadership of Yasuhiro Nakasone, Japan, an economic giant but a military pygmy, is beginning to address the question of improving its national defenses. China, still a potential enemy, is not a military threat to the Soviet Union today. But it looms as an awesome danger for the future because of its one billion people and enormous resources. As historical determinists, the Soviets look at events with the long term in mind. For them, threats in the future are problems in the present.

Andropov can boast of great gains for the Soviet Union in the Third World, but his position with the world's major powers must give him pause. Mao Zedong's military manual called for isolating the cities by capturing the countryside. Andropov's policy is right out of Mao's book. He seeks to strangle the industrial West by cutting off its supply of key resources from the Third World. This strategy might work in the long run, but its most profound immediate effect is to isolate the Soviet Union. Andropov has no allies among the major nations of the world. He faces potential adversaries in Western Europe, Japan, China, Canada, and the United States. Together these countries represent over 60 percent of the world's economy and present the Soviet Union with the grim prospect of having to face powerful enemies on two fronts.

When Andropov totals up the balance sheet of Soviet strengths and weaknesses, he cannot be encouraged. The debits are the tremendous problems he confronts both inside and outside his country. The assets are his military power. Great as they are, his assets are ill-suited to solving his problems.

Andropov is motivated by personal factors as well. He is a man in a hurry. He is ten years older than Brezhnev was when he came to power, eight years older than Khrushchev, 23 years older than Stalin. No one questions his mental alertness, but his physical health is suspect. And while he has taken the reins of the Soviet government, he is not yet firmly in the saddle. He needs a foreign policy initiative.

He has to be looking for ways to deal with his problems or at least to mitigate them. That fact makes the prospects for real peace great. Putting it simply, both sides want peace—the United States because we believe in peace, the Soviets because they need it.

The time is ripe for a deal.

If war in the nuclear age is so disastrous and if economic cooperation is so beneficial, it would seem that striking a deal for peace should be a natural. But that is not the case. The Soviet leaders are not the same kind of people we are. Their political system promotes individuals who view the world in a completely different way and who put an entirely different value on human life.

As Russians, they will weep over the millions of deaths their country suffered in World War II. But as communists, they will defend the actions of a government that killed millions of other Russian citizens. In meeting with Soviet leaders, I often thought of Dr. Jekyll and Mr. Hyde as the warm, friendly Russian of our social conversations transformed himself into a cold, heartless communist as we got down to business. Within minutes, someone who appears to be a warm-hearted pacifist turns into a ruthless thug.

There are many views about how we should deal with the Soviet leadership. At one extreme, we have the superhawks. They argue that because the Soviets are in deep trouble and are out to do us in by any and all means, we should build up military superiority and try to isolate them by cutting off all trade and negotiations. If we do that, they contend, the rotten Soviet economy will eventually collapse, bringing down the communist system with it.

That is an appealing scenario, but not a realistic one. The superhawks are correct in recognizing the Soviets for what they are. But while their premise is correct, their conclusion is wrong. The Soviet system will not collapse.

The Kremlin leaders have never won a free election, but they are masters at getting and keeping power. They have ruthlessly squeezed their people with brutally austere economic policies before, and they will do so again if that is necessary to keep themselves in power. Confrontation and isolation can strengthen a dictatorship. Hard-headed negotiation and contact with the outside world can weaken it.

The superhawks also fail to realize that in a democracy it is impossible to sustain such a policy. The American people and our allies in Europe will shoulder the burden of armaments and bear the risks of military conflict only if they believe their leaders are actively trying to reduce international tensions. The people need to be given hope, for without hope the support for defense expenditures will crumble and the pressure for an ill-considered accommodation with the Soviets will build.

Even if we assume that the superhawks' policy would work and would command the sustained support of the American people, we would still be wrong to adopt it. It is irresponsible for the world's two greatest military powers not to have maximum communication with each other and not to try to negotiate their disputes. This would put our relations in a highly combustible atmosphere of semi-belligerency, with both sides building up armaments without restraint while firing salvos of hot rhetoric. Our interests would inevitably rub together in the powder kegs of the world like the Middle East, possibly sending off the spark which would ignite a nuclear war.

Sir William Slim, a Governor-General of Australia and one of Britain's greatest generals in World War II, made this point in a conversation with me 30 years ago. He was a dedicated anti-communist, but he was also a realist. He believed even then, when the United States had overwhelming nuclear superiority over the Soviet Union, that we should move from confrontation toward negotiation. He told me, "We must break the ice. If we don't break it, we will all get frozen into it so tight that it will take an atom bomb to break it."

In contrast to the superhawks, we have the superdoves at the other extreme. They argue that the Soviet Union fears the United States and arms only because we arm. They excuse virtually every instance of Soviet aggression, from the Cuban missile crisis to the invasion of Afghanistan, on the basis of the Kremlin's need to feel safe from an aggressive West. They contend that if we reassure them that we want peace, they will cease to prepare for war. They say that if we set a peaceful example—by cutting our defense budget—the Soviets will do likewise.

They are wrong. By portraying the Soviet Union as a defensive power beset by foes on all sides, they are doing the same thing Abraham Lincoln wryly accused his political opponents of doing when they twisted his policy statements to serve their purposes: "Turning a horse chestnut into a chestnut horse." A major nuclear power is not threatened by Afghan tribesmen and a country fearful of invasion by its European neighbors does not project its military power into southern Africa and the western hemisphere.

President Carter, with the best of intentions, followed the advice of the superdoves until the Soviets invaded Afghanistan. He cancelled, delayed, or cut back one after another of our arms procurement programs and made a series of conciliatory gestures toward the Soviets. The Kremlin leaders reacted by increasing their arms programs and pushing forward with their armed conquests.

Unlike the superhawks, the superdoves do not recognize the Soviets for what they are. Their argument is flawed at its premise and leads to a dangerous conclusion. We do not have to convince the Soviet leaders that we want peace. They know that. What we need to do is convince them that they cannot win a war. If we take the superdoves' advice, war would become more likely because the risks for an aggressor would be less.

There is also a third group—the defeatists. They argue that we are "better red than dead." They look with horror upon the awesome power of nuclear weapons, see communism as the wave of the future, and conclude that we are better off capitulating quietly. They have little faith in the strength of Western ideals, and value them still less.

What they fail to recognize is that there is a third choice. We can be alive and free.

To keep the peace and defend our freedom, we need to adopt a policy of hard-headed detente. "Detente" has become a notorious codeword. The debate over the word has become so charged with emotion that substance gives way to semantics. We must therefore be clear about what hard-headed detente is and what it is not.

Hard-headed detente is a combination of detente with deterrence. It is not an entente, which is an agreement between powers with common interests, nor is it a synonym for appeasement. It does not mean that the United States and the Soviet Union *agree*. Rather it means that we profoundly *disagree*. It provides a means of peacefully resolving those disagreements that can be resolved, and of living with those that cannot.

Hard-headed detente must be based on a strength of arms and strength of will sufficient to blunt the threat of Soviet blackmail. This should be combined with a mixture of prospective rewards for good behavior and penalties for bad behavior that gives the Soviet Union a positive incentive to keep the peace rather than break it. We must make it clear to the Soviets through our strength and our will that when they threaten our interests, they are risking war. If we simultaneously engage them in a process of resolving our differences where possible, we can turn their attention toward the promise of peace.

There are those who say that detente was merely an attempt to contain the Soviet Union by tying it down in "a delicate web of interdependence." Hard-headed detente as we practiced it did not rely on anything so flimsy. We were prepared to stop Soviet aggression, direct and indirect, not only with diplomatic pressures, but also military ones. We did not reassure those who were threatening our interests that we would not use force unless attacked. Instead, we told them that we would do whatever was necessary to defend our interests and those of our allies. What was even more important, they knew we had the will to back up our words. We did not wring our hands when it became necessary to use military force or the threat of force. Our record established our credibility, and the Soviets respected it.

As we practiced it from 1969 through 1974, hard-headed detente worked. During that period, we used a combination of military and diplomatic pressures to block Soviet advances. We were prepared, if necessary, to give direct or indirect military aid to any country they threatened. We also undertook negotiations with the Soviets on a broad range of issues. Some, like arms control and the settlement of World War II debts, were of mutual interest. Others, like the granting of Most Favored Nation status and the purchase of American grain, were of particular interest to the Soviets. That gave us leverage over them. When they threatened our interests, we slowed or suspended those negotiations. When they relented, we proceeded with them.

As a result, not one nation was lost to the Soviet bloc during this period. Under pressure from us, the Soviet Union in 1970 retreated from its attempt to establish a nuclear submarine base at Cienfuegos in Cuba and from its effort, through Syria, to topple King Hussein of Jordan. It backed away from its support of India's attempt to gobble up West Pakistan in 1971. It abandoned its threat to send Soviet forces into the Middle East during the Arab-Israeli war of 1973.

On the eve of the summit meeting in 1972, we ordered the bombing and mining of Haiphong in order to stop the North Vietnamese offensive. Those who did not understand hard-headed detente thought it would torpedo the summit. They were wrong. It strengthened our hand and helped pave the way for a broad range of agreements.

After this initial success, detente is widely thought to have failed. Detente did not fail, but Congress between 1974 and 1977 and the Carter Administration between 1976 and 1980 failed to implement it in a hard-headed way. Detente without deterrence is a sure-fire recipe for retreat and defeat.

In Southeast Asia, the Congress cut Administration requests for military aid to South Vietnam by half in 1974 and another third in 1975. Also, by passing the War Powers Act and resolutions banning the use of American air power in Indochina, the Congress denied the President the power to enforce the Paris peace accords. The Soviet Union at the same time increased its military aid to North Vietnam. Indochina was lost because the Congress would not allow the United States to do as much for its allies as the Soviet Union did for theirs. This pattern was repeated in Angola in 1975.

Between 1968 and 1975, the Congress cut a total of $40 billion from the defense budgets submitted by the White House. Beginning in 1977, the Carter Administration compounded the problem by unilaterally cutting back on U.S. weapons programs. During this same period, the Soviet Union continued and accelerated its arms buildup. It was inevitable that the Soviet Union would move from strategic parity with the United States in 1974 to a position of decisive superiority in land-based nuclear weapons, the situation that confronted President Reagan when he took office in 1981.

President Carter had tried to practice detente without deterrence. The results were a disaster. The Soviets expanded their domination in the Arabian Peninsula, in southern Asia, in Africa, and in Latin America. The lesson is clear. We can influence Soviet policies but only if we recognize that they will react to our policies. If we block their advances, they will choose restraint and negotiate. If we give an inch, they will take a thousand miles.

The Soviet Union and its apologists are quick to blame the United States for the demise of detente. There is fault on both sides, but far more on the Soviet side.

The practice of hard-headed detente requires the use of both the carrot and the stick. When the Congress refused to grant the Soviet Union Most Favored Nation status, it took away the carrot. Its cuts in the defense budget coupled with President Carter's cancellations and delays of major arms programs left us with a weak stick.

But it was the Soviets who put the nails in the coffin of detente. They destroyed detente by their support of the North Vietnamese offensive in South Vietnam that violated the Paris peace agreements and by their expansionism throughout the Third World. When they invaded Afghanistan, the Soviets made it impossible for President Carter to get SALT II approved by the Senate, and at the same time gave those who opposed detente an effective political issue.

President Reagan has restored the policy of deterrence. He has initiated a major buildup in our military forces in order to reestablish the balance of power, and he has made it clear that he will intervene with those forces to defend our interests and those of our allies and friends. The Soviets as a result have made no geopolitical gains since he came to office.

The President has won Soviet respect with his actions. By standing up to the Soviets, he has made them eager to sit down with him at the negotiating table. This puts him in an ideal position from which to open a new relationship with the Soviet Union that will advance the cause of real peace.

This new relationship must address the two dangers confronting us. We must avoid war, and we must avoid defeat. Defeat can come in war, but the greater danger is that it will come without war, through Soviet adventurism, intimidation, and blackmail. If we lull ourselves into a sense of security while the Soviets take over one country after another, we will wake up one day to find the global balance of power weighted fatally against us.

War can come from five principal sources. It could result if the military superiority of an aggressive power were to go unchallenged. It could result if a leader were to miscalculate what actions by him would provoke a military response from his opposite number. It could result if the major powers were drawn in on opposite sides of a war between minor powers. It could result if a nuclear missile were to be launched accidentally. It could result if a madman were to capture power and embark on an aggressive war.

There is little that we can actively do to prevent the last danger from coming about. But a renewed policy of hard-headed detente can reduce the other dangers greatly. Today, hard-headed detente requires us to restore fully the military balance of power and at the same time to negotiate meaningful arms control agreements. It requires us to use the West's economic power, through strictly regulated East-West trade, to give the Soviets an incentive for peace. And it requires us to establish a process of negotiation and summitry that will weave these strands together into the fabric of real peace.

Restoring the military balance. Our first goal must be to take the profit out of war. Aggressors wage war if they think they can gain something by it. To deter war we must remain powerful enough so that potential aggressors will conclude that they stand to lose far more than they could possibly gain from war. Thus it is essential that we restore the military balance of power.

There are those who say that in the nuclear age it does not matter if one side has a margin of superiority over the other. This reasoning overlooks the diametrically opposed purposes of the United States and the Soviet Union. The United States is a defensive power. When we have used force or threatened to use it, we have done so for defensive, not offensive purposes. If we had so chosen we could have ruled the world immediately after World War II. Instead, we helped rebuild it. Since then, we have gone to war twice, in Korea and in Vietnam. Both times it was for the purpose of defending other nations from aggression by the Soviet Union and its allies.

The Soviet Union is an admittedly and avowedly offensive power. Its leaders' stated goal is world domination, and they have been pursuing that end by every means at their disposal. The Soviet Union does not arm itself for defensive reasons. The leaders in the Kremlin stand behind the aggressors in virtually every one of the world's hotspots and have instigated every postwar confrontation between the superpowers.

This divergence in our aims puts the question of whether military superiority matters in a new light. Winston Churchill understood that difference. In 1946, when only the United States knew how to make the atomic bomb, he commented, "No one in any country has slept less well in their beds because this knowledge and the method and the raw materials to apply it, are at present largely in American hands. I do not believe we should all have slept so soundly had the positions been reversed and if some communist or neo-fascist state monopolized for the time being these dread agencies."

History has borne out the truth of Churchill's insight. For 30 years, from the end of World War II to the mid-1970s, the United States had nuclear superiority. This was the principal factor that deterred the Soviets from launching a war in Europe. When our superiority was great, it also served as a powerful deterrent to Soviet aggression and adventurism in other regions. Superiority in the hands of a defensive power is a guarantee of peace; superiority in the hands of an offensive power is a threat to peace. The danger of defeat without war also increases because the means for nuclear blackmail are given to those who would use it.

Today the United States no longer has the credible nuclear superiority to deter Soviet aggression. While we are still ahead in sea- and air-based missiles, the Soviet Union has in the last ten years acquired decisive superiority in the most powerful and accurate nuclear weapons—land-based missiles. They have a first-strike capability—the ability to destroy virtually all of our land-based missiles in a first strike while having enough left over to destroy our cities. The United States does not have a first-strike capability and has no plans to obtain one.

There are those who say that any such advantage in the nuclear age is meaningless. After all, they argue, even if the Soviet Union destroyed all of our land-based missiles in a first strike, the United States could retaliate by launching its submarine- and bomber-based missiles. Therefore the Soviets would never launch the first strike to begin with.

This overlooks the perilous situation in which an American President could find himself. After a Soviet first strike, the United States would not have the capability of taking out the Soviet Union's remaining land-based missiles. Very few of our strategic bombers can get through Soviet air defenses. Our sea-based missiles can only be used against cities because they do not have the power or accuracy to take out Soviet land-based missiles.

The President's only possible response to a first strike would be to take out Soviet cities. But the Soviets, knowing that they could retaliate in kind, would hardly find such a threat believable. A threat to commit mutual suicide is not a credible policy, let alone a moral one.

However frightening that scenario might be, the real danger is more profound. There are two reasons why any Soviet leader would be reluctant to initiate a nuclear war. The Soviets have never tested their nuclear weapons under wartime conditions. They have a first-strike capability in theory. But the theory relies on the execution of their military plans with split-second timing and precision accuracy during the chaos of war. Military men, who are by nature cautious, would be hesitant to go to war if a minute technical error could lead to devastating defeat. And while the Soviets want to dominate the world, they want to do so without war. They do not want to rule a world of destroyed cities and dead bodies.

The greater danger is that, knowing we have no credible response to their clear superiority in land-based missiles, they will be emboldened at other levels. They will tend to be more adventurous in Asia, Africa, the Middle East, and Latin America and more intimidating in their approach toward Western Europe. They can use the threat of their potential power to dominate the world through nuclear blackmail.

We cannot expect to regain the nuclear superiority we had for 30 years, but the least we must do is deny superiority to the Soviets. The MX missile will help to achieve that goal. It is powerful and accurate enough to take out Soviet land-based missiles. The program President Reagan has asked Congress to approve will not provide us with a first-strike capability because we do not plan to build enough MX missiles to take out all of the Soviet Union's land-based missiles. But it at least begins to rectify the military balance of power. Equally important, if war comes, the MX missile will give an American President some option other than an attack on Soviet cities.

The burden of building up our armed forces will not be light but it will be long. As the richest nation in the world, the United States can afford to spend whatever is necessary for our national defense. But restoring the military balance does not mean that what the Pentagon wants the Pentagon gets. We cannot and should not tolerate waste, duplication, and inefficiency in the military bureaucracy any more than we would in the social service agencies. Misman-agement not only erodes public support for necessary defense spending, but also reduces our ability to defend our national interests.

Some of America's ablest executives have served as secretary of defense in recent years—Melvin Laird, James Schlesinger, Donald Rumsfeld, Harold Brown, and Caspar Weinberger. They can testify to the fact that keeping Pentagon costs under control is an almost impossible task. The secretary of defense often finds himself in the unenviable position of being the ringmaster of a three-ring circus in which the services turn somersaults competing for the attention and dollars of the Administration and Congress. Each service chief understandably believes that what is best for his service is best for the nation. We need a strong Navy, a strong Army, and a strong Air Force. But the Congress and the taxpayers should not and will not support unnecessary duplication of missions and weapon systems.

As President Eisenhower, no dewy-eyed dove, once said, "This country could choke itself to death piling up military expenditures just as surely as it can defeat itself by not spending enough for protection."

Arms Control. The issue of arms control cannot be separated from the question of national security. They are intimately intertwined. Realistically conducted, arms control negotiations can contribute to real peace. Naively pursued, they can increase the risk of war.

Arms control can serve four major purposes.

A properly negotiated agreement can help create the strategic stability that could reduce the chances of war. Strategic instability results when either side or both sides deploy weapons with first-strike capability. This creates a temptation to use these weapons to gain a decisive advantage. The danger is greatest if these weapons themselves are vulnerable to a first strike because in a crisis a leader would be tempted to use his arsenal before he loses it. Any arms control agreement between the United States and the Soviet Union must be based on true equality and must assure strategic stability. Neither can be secure unless both feel secure.

An arms control agreement could reduce the costs of defense for both the United States and the Soviet Union. President Reagan's proposal in the Strategic Arms Reduction Talks calls for each side to dismantle part of its nuclear arsenal and to curb the deployment of even more accurate land-based missiles. If the Soviets accept this approach, it would stop not only the spiral of the arms race but also that of the defense budget.

Achieving arms control is a political imperative. Western leaders will be unable to mobilize public support behind the defense spending necessary to keep up our deterrent unless they have a credible policy of negotiating arms control. The current debate over the production of the MX missile demonstrates this vividly.

Arms control between the superpowers is the first step in controlling nuclear proliferation. Preventing the spread of nuclear weapons technology to other countries is in the interest of both the United States and the Soviet Union. If scores of minor powers acquire nuclear weapons, the chances are great that one will someday use them in a crisis in one of the world's hotspots. Nuclear proliferation could turn out to be the spark that explodes the global nuclear tinderbox. To stop it the superpowers must work together. Only if they succeed in capping their own nuclear buildup can they have any influence over smaller powers that are thinking of developing nuclear weapons.

But while weighing the potential benefits of arms control, we must recognize the hard reality that it will improve the chances for peace only under certain conditions.

An arms control agreement will not contribute to peace unless we reduce the political differences that can lead to war. Avid arms control proponents reject the concept of linking arms control negotiations to political issues. But linkage is a fact of international life. It was the Soviet invasion of Afghanistan that destroyed the chances for Senate approval of SALT II. This was linkage in action, not just in theory.

We should not pursue arms control as an end in itself. It is dangerous to assume that any arms control agreement is better than none. If an agreement is to reduce the risk of war, it must advance six goals.

First, it must create a true balance between the superpowers. All arms control treaties are not created equal, and any we sign must be based on equality. Equality in numbers is important, but numbers should not be the sole measure of equality. For the United States to have an equal number of weapons as the Soviet Union is not enough if the Soviets alone are allowed to retain their present first-strike capability. We should set the number and size of missiles and the number of warheads so that each side has the same military capability in both strategic and medium-range weapons.

Second, it must not allow either superpower to have a credible first-strike capability. If both were to have this capability, each would be strongly tempted in a crisis to preemptively attack the strategic forces of the other. What would be worse, if an agreement gave superiority in first-strike weapons to an offensive power like the Soviet Union, it would actually increase the danger of war and of defeat without war.

We should formally offer to share any technology we develop for a space-based missile defense system with the Soviet Union or any other nation that joins us in seeking meaningful arms control. If all nations could deploy the system at once, none would suspect another of wanting to use it as a shield for an attack.

Third, it must provide the means for each side to verify the compliance of the other. We have relied in the past on satellite photography and other national means of verification. But advances in military technology now require that we settle for nothing less than on-site inspection. The Soviets have always rejected such provisions. We must make them understand that the Administration will only be able to muster the two-thirds Senate majority needed for ratification of a treaty if we have absolute confidence that both sides will carry out its provisions.

Fourth, it must restrict the testing of new missile technology that would destabilize the strategic balance. Technology is advancing faster than the superpowers can negotiate controls on the weapons it produces. The danger is that missile accuracy will advance to the point that neither side will have a nuclear deterrent that can survive a first strike. If we limit the testing of new missiles, we can prevent their deployment, because no country would stake its survival on missiles that had not been flight-tested.

Fifth, it must reduce, not just limit, the nuclear arsenals of the superpowers. The United States has proposed such reductions several times, but the Soviet Union has always rejected the idea. The only conceivable reason for each superpower to maintain its nuclear stockpile at today's levels is that the other superpower is doing so. Through arms control agreements, we can retire the aging and obsolete missiles on both sides and reduce the numbers of new missiles as well.

Sixth, it should allow for the implementation of the Scowcroft Commission's recommendation to replace fixed, land-based, multi-warhead missiles with mobile, single-warhead ones. It takes at least two warheads detonated simultaneously to destroy a land-based missile in its silo. If both sides had equal numbers of single-warhead missiles, neither would have enough warheads to launch a successful first strike against the other. If these missiles were mobile, it would make the success of such an attack so doubtful that one side would never risk attacking the other.

The proposal to freeze the nuclear arsenals of the United States and the Soviet Union at current levels is fatally flawed because it fails to meet these six criteria. Its proponents say that their goals are to achieve meaningful arms control and to reduce the danger of war. Their intentions are good, but their judgment is not. If we were to negotiate a nuclear freeze, its effect would be just the opposite of what they expect.

A nuclear freeze would increase the danger of war because it would leave the Soviet Union, an offensive power, with an unquestionable first-strike capability. It would destroy any chance for meaningful arms reductions because it would eliminate the incentives for the Kremlin leaders to negotiate.

The history of the negotiations that led to the 1972 SALT I treaty limiting defensive nuclear weapons illustrates this point. The Soviets already had begun to deploy an anti-ballistic missile system. When completed, it would protect their command centers and missile bases from a nuclear attack. We countered this by asking the Congress to approve funding for an ABM system for the United States. Our critics charged that we were escalating the arms race and destroying the chances for an arms control agreement. Only after intensive lobbying were we able to get the Senate, by a margin of just one vote, to go along with the proposal.

The approval of the ABM program made SALT I possible. It was in the Soviets' interest to stop us from going forward with our system because our technology was better than theirs. They were therefore willing to pay a price to stop us. But if we had lost the Senate vote, I would have had to ask Brezhnev to give up his ABM system without getting anything in return. He would have just laughed in my face.

The Soviets are not philanthropists. Nor are they fools. They are tough, ruthless negotiators who will give nothing for nothing. In negotiating with them, we cannot get something from them unless we have something to give to them.

The greatest threat to peace today is the Soviet arsenal of strategic land-based missiles. It gives them a first-strike capability. We have nothing in our arsenal to counter this. They will have no incentive to reduce that threat through arms control negotiations unless we have a weapons system in place or in production that would at least in part match their capability. That is why it is essential for us to go forward with the MX missile. Without it, we will never be able to reach an agreement based on any semblance of equality.

The nuclear freeze is a fraud. It is a simple answer to a complex problem. We cannot expect to achieve all our goals in one negotiation, but no agreement we sign should freeze them beyond our reach.

Negotiating an arms control agreement that will contribute to real peace will take years. It is fatuous to suggest that such an agreement could be struck through a quick telephone call between an American President and Andropov. We will not be able to reach all of our goals for restoring strategic equality, increasing stability, and reducing the size of the nuclear arsenals in time for a summit meeting in 1984. But we could negotiate a substantial first step toward one or more of these goals and an agreement in principle on the others.

If significant progress is made along these lines before a summit, Presidents Reagan and Andropov when they meet could agree on long-term goals for arms control and establish a step-by-step process for reaching them. New top-level representatives, who would report directly and periodically to the Presidents, should be given the responsibility for negotiating a specific timetable.

The pieces are in place for an arms control breakthrough. The Soviets dealt themselves a strong hand by relentlessly building up their nuclear weaponry in the 1970s. By modernizing our own we have improved our hand through the draw. But we also have an ace in the hole that gives the Soviets an incentive to strike a fair deal: if there must be a nuclear arms race, we will win it through our superior economic strength and advanced technology.

After an agreement is signed, the pundits inevitably speculate about who won and who lost. But for an arms control agreement to contribute to real peace, there should be no losers, only winners. If the agreement is not to our mutual advantage, it will become politically impossible for the losing side to implement it. Unless both sides reap benefits, the process will falter.

Once we conclude arms control agreements, we must do everything they allow us to because we can be sure the Soviet Union will do so. Opponents of arms control claim that SALT I allowed the Soviets to gain nuclear superiority. The facts prove the contrary. In 1972, programs were under way to develop the B-1 bomber, the Trident II submarine, and the MX, cruise, and Minuteman III missiles. It was the Congress, not SALT I, that delayed these programs. Forty billion dollars were lopped off

Administration defense budgets between 1968 and 1975. This mistake was compounded by President Carter. In his first years in office, he cancelled the B-1, delayed the MX and cruise missiles, shut down the Minuteman III production line, and cancelled the neutron bomb. The Soviets, not surprisingly, did everything SALT I permitted, stretching some provisions in the process. If we had followed a similar policy, there would be no land-based missile gap today.

While we must seek arms control agreements, we must not overestimate what they can accomplish. A bad agreement will increase the risk of war. Not even the best agreement imaginable would solve all our problems. If the United States and the Soviet Union cut their nuclear arsenals in half, a goal that is beyond the wildest dreams of even the most optimistic arms control negotiator on either side, we would still have enough weapons to destroy each other many times over. If we were to make such drastic arms reductions, a nuclear war would be just as devastating as it would be today.

If we are to reduce the risk and danger of war, we must leapfrog the sterile arms control debate and go to the heart of the problem: the political differences between the United States and the Soviet Union and the policies we can initiate that will deter the Soviets from resorting to war to resolve those differences.

Incentives for Peace. Only when deterrence is assured can detente be effective. If the Soviets realize that aggression will not pay, they will have no choice but to behave with restraint. We can then reinforce the effect of the fear of war by providing them with the rewards of peace. Real peace requires a policy that has incentives for peace as well as disincentives for war.

Our economic power dwarfs theirs because our economic system works and theirs does not. The NATO allies and Japan outproduce the Soviet Union and its Warsaw Pact allies by a ratio of over three to one. Trade between our systems can give them an economic stake in peace and lead to greater Soviet restraint.

The Soviets need us. We know this, they know it, and we should make use of it. They are more economically dependent on us than we are on them. We largely trade Western technology for Soviet raw materials. The Soviets need access to our know-how if their economy is to grow through the end of the century. If necessary, we can go elsewhere to buy their products, but they have no alternative supplier for ours. This gives us leverage over them. We should use it to further the cause of real peace by stamping our goods with a political price tag as well as an economic one.

We should have no illusions about what trade can accomplish. Trade by itself will not produce peace or prevent war. Some contend that if we trade more with the Soviet Union, they will be less aggressive. But the Kremlin leaders cannot be bought off by trade. In the late 1970s they showed us that they would both trade and invade. At the other extreme, some contend that the increase in Soviet-American trade in the early years of detente helped fuel Soviet expansionism. This claim is preposterous. The level of trade was minuscule then; it could not possibly have affected Soviet military power. Economic relations can never substitute for deterrence. If properly implemented, they can reinforce it.

Lenin contemptuously remarked that capitalists were so short-sightedly greedy that they would sell the communists the rope by which they themselves would someday hang. Unfortunately, some Western businessmen fit the bill. They would sell the Soviets not only rope, but also the scaffolding and a how-to book for the hangman. By refusing to look beyond the bottom line, they blithely ignore the military power the Soviets are massing on the front line.

Trade should be expanded only in ways that serve our interests. This means that we must not sell the Soviets goods and technology that directly contribute to their military capability. It also means that our trade must not be at subsidized prices or on easy credit terms. The rule should be "trade, not aid."

Beyond this, we should expand our economic contacts. We should sell them rope, if they want to buy it, but do so in a way that binds their hands and prevents them from reaching out to further their domination. The more we engage the Soviet Union in an intricate network of commercial relations, the more we increase its stake in peace—and also increase its incentive to maintain good relations with us.

When the Russians marched into Afghanistan, the United States was reduced to boycotting the Olympics in Moscow and imposing a grain embargo that was meaningless because other suppliers were ready to rush in to fill the gap. We would have had more leverage if we had been trading in more things the Russians wanted.

Our leverage with trade will be minimal unless our allies in Europe and Japan join with us in developing a common policy. Acting together economically, the West is a powerful giant. Acting separately, it is an impotent giant.

For economic leverage to be effective, it must be substantial. We must have something significant to give and also to take back. We need both the carrot and the stick.

The Soviet leaders want what the West produces, and they are willing to give up something to get it. The key is to make it very clear to them that there is an iron link between their behavior and the West's willingness to make the trade deals they hope for.

Soviet leaders reject explicit linkage, whether to trade or to arms control negotiations. They will not adopt the principle of linkage, but they will adapt to the fact of it. We must make them understand that linkage is a fact of international life. The American people will not support arms control and trade initiatives with the Soviet Union at a time when it is engaging in aggressive actions that threaten our interests.

For linkage to work, however, it must be done privately. We should not make statements or take actions that will make the Soviets lose face publicly. For example, Jewish emigration from the Soviet Union increased from 400 in 1968 to nearly 35,000 in 1973 as a result of the private pressure of our Administration. Congress then passed a law—the Jackson-Vanik amendment—which put the Russians on the spot publicly by tying trade to emigration policy. The number of Jews allowed to emigrate was cut in half the following year.

Peaceful trade is totally inconsistent with the Soviet Union's aggressive policies. I once heard President Eisenhower remark, "We should sell the Russians anything that they can't shoot back." When they use their economic ties with the West to finance their expansionist policies, the Soviets are in effect shooting back our assistance. The West cannot be so foolish as to subsidize its own destruction.

During World War II, the United States recognized the importance of economic power by setting up a Board of Economic Warfare. Today we need a Foreign Economic Policy Board to concert the use of our economic power. It should answer directly to the President because only he would be able to knock heads together when the bureaucrats in the various agencies involved with foreign economic policy engage in Washington's favorite sport: fighting for turf. Policies governing trade, foreign aid, loans, and support of international lending agencies must be coordinated to serve American foreign policy interests. A process should also be established for enlisting the cooperation of the private sector in serving those interests. It makes no sense for the government to cut off aid to hostile nations while American banks continue to make huge loans to those same nations.

Trade is not a panacea. It does not solve all our problems. Nothing can remove the burden of deterrence from our shoulders. Our policies must be designed to take the profit out of war, but we should also put more profit into peace. On these two pillars—deterrence and detente—we can build a structure of real peace.

Summit Meetings. Summitry between the leaders of the superpowers is indispensable in the pursuit of real peace. It is at the summit that we bring together the various strands of hard-headed detente. This is a delicate exercise that we should undertake only if progress on resolving substantive issues is assured. No American President should go to the summit unless he knows what is on the other side of the mountain.

Rushing into a quickie summit just so the leaders of the superpowers can get acquainted would be a stupid and devastating mistake. Such a summit might temporarily improve the atmospherics of our relations, but little else. The famous "spirit of Geneva," as well as the spirits of other Soviet-American summits at Camp David, Vienna, and Glassboro, was illusory. When a summit is all spirit and no substance, the spirit evaporates fast.

Andropov is understandably reluctant to schedule a summit at a time when it might help President Reagan win reelection. But with the resurgence of the American economy and the President's rise in the polls, Andropov is caught between a rock and a hard place. If he deliberately delays a summit until after the election, he will find himself facing a President with a new mandate and a stronger bargaining position. Andropov needs a summit before the American election more than President Reagan does. We should not give it to him on the cheap.

The words coming out of Moscow seem to indicate that they would like a summit. Their deeds would indicate otherwise. Some pundits have seized upon certain "signals" they interpret as being positive. But permitting a half-dozen Pentacostalists to emigrate, making some semantic concessions on human rights at the Madrid conference, allowing progress toward expanded cultural and diplomatic ties, and lifting martial law in Poland while transferring most of its repressive features to the civil code are not actions that deserve serious consideration. Real peace is too important for tokenism. Unless substantial progress is assured on arms control and on reducing Soviet adventurism in Central America, we should not agree to hold a summit.

If the summit produces too little, there are two dangers. The first is disillusionment. The first Reagan-Andropov meeting will receive enormous worldwide attention. Expectations will be high. If the summit fails to live up to them, the letdown will be catastrophic. The disappointment could lead both sides to give up on the process of peace and increase preparations for war.

The second danger is euphoria. Sometimes simply the fact of a summit gives many in the West unrealistic hopes for the future. They mistakenly believe that we have reached the end of the journey to peace rather than just made a beginning. This makes it more difficult for Western leaders to gain public support for the decisive actions and strong military forces that are needed to make hard-headed detente work.

Summits must produce more than tokenism. They cannot make miracles, but they can make progress. As Churchill once said, "It would, I think, be a mistake to assume that nothing can be settled with Soviet Russia unless or until everything is settled."

The first Soviet-American summit in Moscow in 1972 was scheduled only after the Soviets agreed to the Berlin settlement in 1971. We believed that if we could reach an agreement on an issue that had plagued East-West relations for 30 years and had at times brought us to the brink of war, we could reasonably expect to make progress on other major issues.

Similarly, before we schedule the next summit, personal representatives of Presidents Reagan and Andropov should undertake a series of intensive, absolutely confidential negotiations to explore what progress can be made in reaching agreement on major issues. This would be the most promising forum in which to search for some form of accommodation that advances the general interests of both parties by compromising on the specific interests of each. It would allow the two sides to subtly feel out the differing degrees to which various elements of the other party's positions are negotiable, and to try varying combinations of give-and-take.

The summit agenda must be broad. It must include arms control, trade, and conduct in areas where our political differences collide, such as the Middle East, Africa, and Central America. In these preparatory talks, links should be forged between these issues. For example, the

Russians must be made to understand that there is no way the Congress could or should approve arms control or trade agreements reached at a summit when Soviet surrogates continue to try to build another beachhead in Central America.

The Soviets will loudly object to such linkage, but they will understand it. After all, their paranoia about having "friendly" buffer states on their borders puts them in a poor position for objecting to our concern about what happens to our neighbors. President Kennedy drew the line when the Soviets tried to put missiles into Cuba in 1962. I drew the line when they tried to put a nuclear submarine base on Cuba in 1970. President Reagan has drawn the line in El Salvador. He is right to do so. We should make it clear to the Soviets that we will do whatever is necessary to prevent the establishment of another Soviet base in the Americas.

All discussions should proceed on the principle of strict reciprocity. We give them something they want only if they give us something we want. By not capitalizing on our economic power, we have been giving away enormous assets for free. And the Soviets, who are experts at the hoarding and exploiting of power, must certainly view our failure to use our assets as a sign of both stupidity and weakness.

Our primary goal should be to build a new relationship with the Soviets in which we will be able to prevail upon them to cease their aggression. This can only happen when the bilateral relationship with us becomes more important to them than their adventurism.

We must develop a process for annual summits between the leaders of the United States and the Soviet Union. These meetings can both reduce the chances of war and help restrain Soviet behavior.

Regularly scheduled summits allow each leader to take the measure of the other and thus can reduce the possibility of miscalculation during a confrontation. In 1973, on the last night of my second summit with Brezhnev, we had a midnight meeting in San Clemente about the Middle East situation. He tried to push me into agreeing on a settlement that the superpowers would impose on Israel and the other nations of the region. I categorically and firmly resisted this pressure. We went at it toe-to-toe for three hours. After that confrontation, he had to know that we were not bluffing during the Yom Kippur War four months later, when we called an alert of our military forces in response to his threat to send Soviet combat troops into the Middle East.

If the leaders of the superpowers get to know each other, it does not mean they will like each other. But each controls such enormous power that it is vital that they take every possible step to reduce the possibility that either might underestimate the will of the other to defend his nation's interests.

Regular summits will tend to restrain Soviet behavior. As a meeting approaches the Kremlin leaders will be reluctant to do anything that might "poison" the atmosphere and therefore make it more difficult to reach the agreements they want. Brezhnev had an eye on the calendar when he agreed to join us in bringing about a ceasefire in the war between India and Pakistan in 1971. He would have preferred to embarrass the Chinese by allowing his client, India, to gobble up China's client, Pakistan. But he knew the cost would include the cancellation of a summit meeting he wanted. We had made that risk categorically clear to him.

Regular summits that produce concrete results will help the United States and our allies mobilize public support for necessary defense programs. While we should not have a summit simply because our allies and friends favor it, the fact that we will go to the summit when it is properly prepared reassures them. Hope for real peace is essential if the people of the United States as well as Europe are to continue to support the military strength necessary to maintain the foundation of deterrence on which detente rests. There may be occasional spurts of spending when the threat of Soviet aggression seems acute, but over the long haul the absence of hope for peace fuels the forces of appeasement.

Good or bad personal relations at a summit will not have a decisive effect on state relations. But the two cannot be separated. We should not assume that better personal relations will automatically improve bad state relations. Still, poor personal relations will make it more difficult to improve bad state relations, and could even aggravate them.

In negotiating with the Kremlin leaders, an American President should be cordial in personal matters but unyielding in policy matters. As Franklin Roosevelt learned, with tragic consequences for the people of Poland and the other nations behind the Iron Curtain, any President who believes he can get the men of the Kremlin to change their policies by charming them or simply through personal persuasiveness is due for a rude awakening. But while mushy sentimentality should be avoided, a President achieves nothing by bluster and belligerence. The Russians are masters of the bluff and can usually detect that tactic when it is used against them. Bluster and bad manners may intimidate the weak but never the strong. Talking softly while carrying a big stick is the most effective way to deal with the Soviets.

While not decisive, personal relationships can be mar-
ginally important when dealing with the leaders of the
Soviet Union. Before my meeting with Khrushchev in
1959, British Prime Minister Macmillan told me that the
Soviet leaders desperately wanted to be "admitted to the
club"—accepted and respected as major world figures in
their own right and not simply because they control the
great military power of the Soviet Union. The Russian
people are a great people, and the Soviet Union is a great
power. We should agree to admit the Soviet leaders into
the "club," but only if they agree to abide by the rules. It
is a cheap price to pay if it helps restrain Soviet conduct.

We must make the Soviets understand that there is no
way that we would or should admit them to the club if
they continue to act as the moral outlaws of the world.
When they shot down the Korean jetliner, they also shot
down the prospects for quickly improving our relations
in mutually beneficial ways.

Our initial response was to express our outrage in the
strongest moral terms. We should not mince words in
venting our anger because it clarifies the moral issue that
is at the heart of the East-West struggle. But we must
not delude ourselves by thinking that our statements
about morality will have any effect behind the Kremlin
walls. Condemning the Soviet leaders with statements
based on Western ideals about the sanctity of human life
is like making faces at the Sphinx.

Some have understandably urged us to make a stronger
response. They advocate that we break off our diplomatic
relations with the Soviet Union, halt all our bilateral
negotiations, and impose an array of trade sanctions. But
they are overlooking one of the important lessons of this
tragedy. As a vivid example of the danger of accidental
war, it points out the fact that in the nuclear age there

should be more communication between the superpowers rather than less. While this is not the first atrocity committed by the Soviets, the West should seek to make it their last by seizing the moment to implement a strategy for dealing with them. We must develop a policy of hard-headed detente that will convince the Kremlin leaders that they stand to lose far more than they could possibly gain by threatening our interests. We can succeed only if we use the unity the world has found in its moral outrage to forge a strategy for real peace.

A major communist head of state in Eastern Europe recently remarked to me that the last 60 years have seen a curious reversal in the rhetoric of East and West. The communists used to say that capitalism was collapsing, and now the capitalists are saying that communism is collapsing. He then observed, "Perhaps both are wrong."

He was right. We have differences with the Soviets that we will never overcome. We will never condone their conquests and will always oppose their expansionist policies. But we cannot wish them away. They are there, so we have to deal with them. How we deal with them will determine whether we achieve real peace.

We should avoid hot rhetoric, but we should not mince words. If the world is to have real peace, the Soviets must change their aggressive ways. Their persistence in expanding their influence and control by violent means will sooner or later end in war. And the chances are good that such a war will end the world.

Winston Churchill once said, "I cannot forecast to you the action of Russia. It is a riddle wrapped in a mystery inside an enigma; but perhaps there is a key. That key is Russian national interest." Hard-headed detente is not a magic wand that will with one wave instantly make over the ruthless men in the Kremlin. It is a policy that will lead them to cooperate in the search for real peace because it is in their interest to do so.

Hard-headed detente gives the Kremlin leaders a choice between aggression and restraint. If they choose the first, the danger of war will escalate and the burden of arms will become unbearable. The world will be an increasingly perilous place to live in. If they choose the second, we can reduce the risk of war and reap the fruits of real peace. We will still have our conflicts, but these will not lead to war. If we act together, the United States and the Soviet Union can contribute to peace for ourselves and for others. If we continue to act against each other, peace has no chance.

NATO AND JAPAN

In considering the role the United States and Soviet Union must play, we must always bear in mind that other nations, particularly those of Western Europe and Japan, must be part of any effective effort to build a real peace. After all, the struggle between East and West for 35 years has in large part been a struggle over the fate of Europe and Asia.

Given the Soviets' ambitions and strength, Europe cannot have peace and freedom without the United States. But by the same token the U.S. cannot build a lasting peace without Europe. As Franklin Roosevelt said to his war-weary people in 1945, "We have learned that we cannot live alone, in peace." We learned that lesson from fighting the bloodiest war in history, and it is even more true today.

The U.S. is linked with its European allies on a variety of levels. We are largely a composite of European peoples and European ideals. We share values, faiths, and cultural and philosophical heritages with Europe. But what links us most fundamentally is our reverence for liberty, and we realize that the greatest evil of Soviet totalitarianism is that it smothers liberty. Our military alliances and our close economic and cultural relationships are expressions both of our common heritage and our mutual awareness of a common external threat.

That is why Japan, while an Asian rather than a European nation, is as central to the Western alliance as any NATO member. Strategically, along with China it holds the eastern ramparts. Economically, its might is indispensable if we are to have an effective Western economic policy. And practically, it has much to gain from an alliance with the West because it has just as much to lose as the U.S. and the Europeans from further Soviet advances.

The postwar Japanese economic miracle was the result of an unprecedented synthesis of East and West. Japanese creativity, drive, and skill, channelled through Western systems of government and free enterprise, made Japan one of the economic giants of the modern world. The Japanese have reaped the rewards of liberty, and not surprisingly they have shown a growing willingness to defend what they have built.

Americans sometimes have a certain messianic, "We'll save the world" attitude. We believe in our system and way of life and are eager to share both with the rest of the world. Woodrow Wilson did not call on the American people to fight in World War I just to save *America* but to serve the greater goal of making the *world* safe for democracy. We have always been confident that the sheer rightness of our ideals will win out in the end.

We believe the American ideal is still the world's best hope. But the economic and military power of the United States in the world is not as commanding as it once was.

After World War II the U.S. economy accounted for more than half of the world's industrial production. The figure is now less than a third—in part because with our help Japan and West Germany, our adversaries in war, have become our strongest competitors in peace. Our military dominance is also gone. We have lost the strategic edge in land-based missiles to the Soviet Union. To meet the Soviet military challenge we need European forces, deployed through NATO, as well as our own.

The U.S. has played the starring role in the Western alliance for so long that our allies sometimes act as if it is a one-man show. Too often when crises have erupted—in Iran, in Afghanistan, in Central America—our allies have sat back and waited for the U.S. to step forward and respond. This cannot continue. The Europeans and the Japanese need the U.S., and the U.S. needs them. If hardheaded detente is to work, each nation in the industrialized West must realize that we live in a new world which the superpowers alone could destroy in a nuclear war, but in which we need the full participation of all our allies to build a real peace.

NATO, as it prepares for its thirty-fifth anniversary next year, faces an urgent task: it must achieve no less than a new birth of purpose and function. It was formed in 1949 as a deterrent to a Soviet attack across the central plain of Europe, and since then it has been the most successful military alliance in modern history. But what was adequate in 1949 is not adequate to meet the challenges of 1983.

As a military alliance NATO has precise, narrow perimeters. Today it must grow in order to survive: grow not in the sense of adding more members, but by expanding its geographical horizons, deepening its military strength along the front lines, and pulling itself together in the way it uses its economic power, one of its strongest weapons.

Just as a house divided against itself cannot stand, an alliance cannot stand if its periphery is threatened, its military forces inadequate, its members divided on the question of how to use its economic power. NATO is weakened by all of these maladies, and to overcome them it must take a good, hard look at itself. It must refocus, rethink, reappraise, and renew.

A common error in military planning is to prepare for the wars of the future with the strategies and the weapons of the past. Alliances are as prone to making this mistake as are generals and nations. To avoid the pitfall NATO must acknowledge the passing of an era, one in which the greatest likelihood of a Soviet attack was in Europe, and acknowledge the coming of a new era. Today the Soviets, directly or through proxies, have the ability to act virtually anywhere and on virtually any level of military force, from guerrilla insurrection through nuclear attack. We must be able to respond accordingly.

If it is to meet the challenge of the new era, NATO must grow in three distinct ways.

It must strengthen its military power.

America's historic guarantee of Europe's security is questionable today because of our lost strategic superiority. The strategy of the Atlantic alliance was based on the proposition that the U.S. and Europe were militarily linked—that a Soviet attack against Europe would be senseless because of the certainty of a U.S. nuclear response. We now lack a credible deterrent to a Soviet attack on Europe for the same reason we lack a credible deterrent to an attack on the United States. Mutual suicide, again, is not a viable foreign policy.

The so-called trip-wire—the likelihood of massive U.S. nuclear retaliation against a Soviet conventional attack in Europe—is dangerously frayed. Nothing has yet taken its place. With their multiple-warhead SS-20s trained on every military target in Western Europe, the Soviets could hold NATO hostage to the possibility of a successful nuclear first strike. As NATO's new missiles are deployed beginning late this year the theater balance will be gradually corrected. The MX program will begin to restore the strategic balance. But this will still leave a yawning gap in the West's defenses: our substantial weakness in conventional forces.

There is a dangerous military imbalance in Europe that must be corrected across the board, at both the theater nuclear level and the conventional level. The West needs a seamless web of military power in which the fabric will be just as strong wherever and however our opponents try to penetrate it.

Some say a balance between NATO and the Soviet Union in theater nuclear weapons will obviate the need for a conventional buildup. Others say that if NATO restores the conventional balance the new medium-range theater missiles, the Pershing II and the cruise, need not be deployed in Western Europe.

Both these contentions are wrong. The Soviet threat exists at both levels, nuclear and conventional, and the threat must be countered with equal effectiveness at both levels.

Once East-West nuclear forces are stabilized, the incentive for Soviet aggression in Europe using conventional forces will vastly increase because of the Warsaw Pact's decisive advantage on the ground. As matters stand now, NATO could hold out only for a matter of weeks, perhaps days, against such an attack. Combatants in war will always use the ultimate weapon to avoid defeat. Any conventional war stands a good chance of escalating to the nuclear level.

NATO's neglect of its conventional forces has lowered the nuclear threshold and increased the chances of nuclear war in Europe. But the damage is not irreparable. According to a recent study published in the London *Economist* NATO would only have to spend a relatively modest four percent more a year to beef up its conventional forces to levels which could deter a Soviet conventional attack. By thus raising the nuclear threshold, it's worth every cent it would cost.

However, developing the capability to deter a Soviet conventional attack does not mean that NATO could safely accept superiority in nuclear weapons by cancelling deployment of the new Pershing II and cruise missiles.

Even with sufficient NATO forces on the ground, we need theater-level nuclear equality with the Soviet Union. The Russians think of war as war; they do not make polite distinctions between the use of nuclear weapons and conventional weapons. What has been called the "unusability of nuclear weapons" makes them more usable to the Soviet Union than to the West. The Soviet Union has no domestic restraints from a population paralyzed by media reports about the terror of nuclear weapons. It can manipulate the fear of nuclear weapons in the West without being too concerned about the fear of nuclear weapons in the Soviet Union.

If because of NATO's increased conventional forces the Russians launched an attack on the ground and that attack was repulsed, they would be tempted to use their SS-20s against Europe as long as NATO lacked the capacity of striking back at the Soviet Union with medium-range missiles such as the Pershing II and the cruise.

In the short term, before the Warsaw Pact-NATO conventional balance is achieved, renouncing a first strike or cancelling the new medium-range missiles would sound the death knell for NATO. Keeping 200,000 American soldiers in Europe at a time when the Soviet Union had superiority at both the conventional and theater nuclear levels would leave them fatally vulnerable to attack.

Failing to restore the theater nuclear balance would force the President of the United States to withdraw our forces from Europe. Without American troops NATO would disintegrate, leaving to the Soviets the morsel that has tantalized them since World War II: West Germany, a non-nuclear power that could not by itself resist a Soviet attack even for a few days.

Since the end of World War II Germany has been the Soviet Union's primary target in Europe. That is why Andropov's insistence on counting French and British nuclear weapons against his SS-20s is such a patent sham. Both Britain and France maintain their forces for their own defense, not for the defense of others. Nuclear weapons under U.S. control are West Germany's only deterrent against massively superior Soviet conventional forces. Without that deterrent West Germany would be nothing but blackmail bait for the hungry Russian bear.

For 30 years after World War II American strategic superiority, the trip-wire, was enough to deter the Soviets from an attack in Europe. Those days are over. NATO must pick up the slack.

Its first steps in that direction have been costly and controversial. While fear of the Soviet Union helps hold NATO together, fear of a nuclear holocaust among a growing number of Europeans threatens to tear it apart.

Ultimately fear of the Soviets is not enough to sustain the Western alliance. The essence of deterrence is the *belief* in deterrence and the hope that the West's military power is being used as part of an overall plan to prevent military confrontation. Without hope of progress toward real peace NATO's will to resist could collapse. Hard-headed detente will provide that hope; so too will the softening of harsh East-West rhetoric that will inevitably result as the superpowers begin to substitute negotiation for confrontation.

The Western alliance must realize that Soviet advances in the Third World threaten the lifeline of every Western industrial nation. Whether this takes place in Afghanistan, Yemen, Ethiopia, or Angola, it is as much an attack on the Western alliance as would be an assault on Europe itself.

In the third of a century since NATO was founded there have been enormous changes in the nature of the Soviet challenge. In the early postwar years the Soviet Union was dangerous to those on its borders, but it was not yet skilled in the projection of power. As the Soviet Union has grown stronger, however, it has also grown immensely more sophisticated in making its power felt far beyond its borders.

NATO remains a traditional military alliance, its forces deployed to deter a Soviet blitzkrieg across the Elbe but dangerously unprepared for a Soviet thrust toward the Persian Gulf or a maneuver by Cuban proxy forces in Africa. In effect we have built a Maginot Line of nuclear and conventional forces along Western Europe's border, while the Soviet Union has learned to use its forces to go under and around borders. As a result the West is in grave danger of being outflanked.

When NATO was founded Europe was weak at the center but strong on the perimeter. The continent itself had been devastated by World War II, but the great European empires were still in place. Today Europe is strong at the center but vulnerable on the perimeter. If the perimeter is breached, the center will collapse. Soviet advances anywhere around the globe—in Asia, the Persian Gulf, or resource-rich Africa—are as potent a threat to Europe as any conventional attack. The industrialized West, including Japan, will be choked to death if the sources of oil and minerals essential to its economies fall into hostile hands.

Some, including many in Europe who continue to expect the U.S. to carry the ball in crisis after crisis, think it ridiculous to suggest that the West could be defeated in the hinterlands rather than on the front lines. If it were, however, it would not be unprecedented. In the American Civil War some thought the North would win by capturing the capital of the Confederacy. But wiser hands knew differently. The Union would defeat the South not simply by pressing "On to Richmond!" but by cutting it off from the rest of the world by blockading its ports, seizing the Mississippi River, and thus stemming the flow of resources for the Confederate war effort.

This was called the "Anaconda Plan." Although it was derided at first, eventually it helped the North win the war.

The Russians know that there are other ways to defeat Europe besides "On to Bonn!" or "On to Paris!" Theirs is an Anaconda Plan on a much grander scale. Like a giant octopus they might wrap one coil around the oil jugular at the Persian Gulf; another could reach into Africa and cut off the flow to Europe of key raw materials. The West depends on the resources of the developing world to keep its economies and its armies functioning. The Soviets know that depriving the West of these resources could injure it as mortally as a direct military assault.

There are those who say that since the U.S. is the Soviet Union's principal adversary, countering Soviet aggression, especially in the developing world, is Washington's problem. This is a fatal delusion. The U.S. is far more self-sufficient in resources than Europe. While we could get along without the oil of the Persian Gulf, Japan and Europe, with the exception of Britain and the North Sea countries, could not. Europe and Japan have a far greater stake in what happens in Afghanistan, Ethiopia, Yemen, and other Soviet targets in the Gulf than has the United States.

Recently, because of such programs as the rapid deployment force, the United States has improved its ability to act quickly in crises on the other side of the world. While the rapid deployment force is a good idea, too much such power would be too much of a good thing. It might encourage our allies in their tendency to think that the U.S. can do it all. The Europeans have generations of experience in dealing with the nations of Africa and the Mideast. If a crisis that threatens the alliance's interests erupts in the Europeans' backyard, they should be prepared to act on behalf of the alliance. France's playing the lead role in Chad, for instance, is an indispensable factor in stopping the Soviets, through their Libyan proxies, from muscling into central Africa.

The idea that the United States could or should act as the policeman of the world is obsolete. Peace is everybody's business. And real peace will not be built unless everyone does his share in building it and keeping it in good repair.

The United States, Europe and Japan must consolidate and learn to use their economic power. Together we could use our strategic economic edge in the same way the U.S. once used its military edge: to deter Soviet aggression around the world. Separately we are isolated nations the Soviets can deal with individually and even play off against one another. Together we out-produce the Soviet bloc by over three to one. Separately any attempt to deter Soviet aggression with economic power is doomed to failure.

The pipeline fiasco proved this point. The United States' trade with the Soviet Union in 1982 was $2.5 billion; Western Europe's was $40.7 billion. Acting together, we could have had a massive impact on the Soviets. But when the Europeans refused to go along, we found that acting alone amounted to a woefully ineffective gesture.

At present NATO recognizes and is beginning to repair the rips in the fabric of its military deterrent. By failing to unite on economic questions in addition to military ones, the West is denying itself the advantage in an area where it still has superiority over the Soviet bloc. To be united militarily but divided economically courts disaster. But by concerting the use of their economic power the U.S. and its allies can develop a powerful weapon to deter Soviet adventurism, while forging an equally powerful instrument with which to encourage peaceful change within the Soviet bloc.

Economic power can be both our sword and our plowshare. Unfortunately, so far the profound differences that have existed between the members of the Western alliance over the use of economic power have made it a useless weapon in our strategic arsenal. In the future, however, we cannot afford to let any of our weapons go unused. The Soviet Union wages the contest across the entire board, militarily, economically, and ideologically. For the West, meeting the Soviets on each of these fronts is both an opportunity and a necessity.

A U.S. President who goes to the summit with the leader of the Soviet Union should carry with him the chits of the other major industrial powers. When he sits across from his Soviet counterpart it should be as if the leaders of all the nations of the Western alliance were arrayed at his right and left at the negotiating table.

When President Reagan meets Andropov the consensus statement in support of theater nuclear weapons that emerged from the recent Williamsburg summit guarantees that he will hold a stronger hand than he would have otherwise. Now that the economic picture in the United States and Europe is improving another meeting of the Western leaders might produce the agreement on unified economic policies that has proved so elusive in the past few years. Before meeting with our adversaries it is essential that we meet with our allies. The Western powers and Japan should schedule an additional summit before the Soviet-American summit.

Such a show of unity has two advantages. It makes it unmistakably clear to the Soviets that the alliance is sound. It also gives the Europeans a chance to help set the agenda.

The U.S. is far more powerful than it was two decades ago, but relative to the rest of the alliance it has proportionately less power than it once had. That means the alliance as a whole is more powerful than it used to be, but only if it acts as an alliance and not a mutual admiration society composed only of fair-weather friends.

Our alliance should not be like OPEC, a cartel whose fabric is in immediate danger of being rent whenever market conditions make it profitable for one or more members to bolt. The members of the Western alliance must accept that the only kind of action that will have an effect in the struggle with the Soviet Union is unified action—that in matters of East-West relations it is in *each nation's* interest to serve the *alliance's* interest.

This applies not only to the Europeans but to the United States as well. Europe's military contribution is as indispensable as ours; along with Japan its combined economy is greater than ours. Yet on matters affecting the whole alliance American Administrations have too often acted first and consulted with our allies second, and then only as an afterthought. By virtue of our position as the "leader of the Western world" we have sometimes treated the Europeans as poor relations who were expected to follow us meekly down any path we chose to take.

The Europeans have centuries of experience in leadership. Every one of our political institutions is based on European models or theories. They know the way the world works. The fact that we are the West's most powerful nation does not mean that we have a monopoly on wisdom. America needs Europe not just because of its economic power and potential military power but because of its brain power. Real peace is too important to settle for anything less than the best thinking the Western world can mobilize to achieve our goal.

CHINA

Before negotiating with our adversaries we should develop a consensus on key issues with our allies and friends. This is true of Japan and the nations of Western Europe. It is also true of the People's Republic of China. That is why, apart from other issues, President Reagan's meeting with Chinese leaders next spring is vitally important.

Our relationship with China is a key element of our strategy vis-a-vis the Soviet Union. Many in the United States opposed our China initiative 11 years ago because of their opposition to communism in any form. They contended that since both China and Russia are communist powers, we should treat both as potential adversaries. They failed to recognize a profound difference. The Soviet Union threatens us. China does not. If we had not undertaken that initiative and China had been forced back into the Soviet orbit, the threat to the West of Soviet communist aggression would be infinitely greater than it is today.

When I travelled to China in 1972 to meet Mao and Zhou, it was in the interests of both nations that we forge a new link based not on common ideals, which bind us to our Western allies, but on common interests. Both sides recognized that despite our profound philosophical differences we had no reason to be enemies and a powerful reason to be friends: our mutual interest in deterring the Soviet threat.

That threat is much greater today than it was then. The Soviet Union is ahead of the United States in strategic, land-based missiles. In addition it has every major military installation in China targeted with its powerful SS-20s. The 50 Soviet divisions on the Chinese border, the Soviets' invasion of Afghanistan, and Soviet domination of Southeast Asia threaten China with the possibility of encirclement, a prospect it did not face in 1972.

Both China and the United States should increase their military strength to deter Soviet aggression in Asia. An important goal in any talks between the Reagan Administration and China's pragmatic new leadership should be to generate more action and less talk about joint defensive efforts. Public posturing about our military cooperation only irritates the Soviets. It does not frighten or deter them.

The relationship between the U.S. and China, however, must be more that simply a strategic and military one. Many, by speaking flippantly of "playing the China card," imply that one billion Chinese are just an ace in the hole for the U.S. to deploy against the Russians whenever it suits our interests. This trivializes a profoundly important relationship. If two nations treat their relationship like a game of cards, what they build will be a house of cards that will collapse when hit with the first ill wind.

I believed in 1972 and still believe that even if there were no Soviet threat, the world's most prosperous nation and the world's most populous nation must work together if we are to succeed in building a safer, better world.

Such a relationship, based on the prospects for long-term benefit rather than the dictates of short-term expediency, will require careful tending. It should not be allowed to founder on minor obstacles such as textile imports or the fate of Chinese defectors, or even more difficult ones such as the Taiwan question.

When President Reagan and the Chinese leaders meet they are certain to find that the interests that draw them together are infinitely more important than the differences that could drive them apart.

We should welcome and not fear China's attempt to reduce tensions with the Soviet Union. Those who cynically observe that it might serve our interests for the two communist giants to fight each other are out of their minds. A war between two major powers in the nuclear age would inevitably escalate into a world war. Consequently it is in our interests for China and the Soviets to try to reduce tensions between them which could result in war. It is equally in China's interests for the U.S. and the Soviet Union to try to reduce tensions between *them* which could result in war.

On the other hand, both China and the United States should approach any negotiations with the Russians with hard-headed realism. Neither China nor the U.S. threatens the other. When the Soviet Union adopts this same policy toward both of us, only then will progress be made in reducing tensions.

China and the United States are held together now by a common fear of the Soviet Union. But as is true in NATO or any other formal arrangement among nations, fear alone is not enough to sustain our new relationship. Fear is the result of the actions of other nations, such as the Soviet Union. When fear is our only incentive to stay together, in effect we leave our fate in the hands of others.

A relationship will last only if we have compelling reasons to work together apart from fear of what others do. If our relationship is based on economic cooperation, our fate remains in our hands. If our relationship is to grow, in the next ten years Sino-U.S. economic cooperation can and should become at least as important as our military cooperation.

Our economic relationship is a natural one. China is still a developing nation; it needs rapid economic progress. The two areas where its need is the greatest are the two in which the United States is best able to provide: agriculture and technology. The progress in the first ten years of our new relationship has been substantial—our trade with China is twice as great as our trade with the Soviet Union. The increase in U.S.-China trade in the next ten years could be dramatically higher.

Closer economic ties between China and the U.S. have strategically significant implications. A weak China invites aggression. China cannot become stronger militarily unless it becomes stronger economically. A strong China will be a problem for the Soviet Union long before it is a problem for us. In the foreseeable future we have more to fear from a China that is too weak—and therefore subject to Soviet intimidation—than one that is too strong.

What is needed in our economic relations is not a Mao-style "great leap forward," which has connotations of unreality, but a *new* leap forward, based on the realization that increased Sino-U.S. cooperation could prove to be the decisive factor in ensuring the health and growth of our relationship in the future. Apart from the security aspect, China, with its enormous natural and human resources, will inevitably become an economic giant in the next century and potentially one of America's most important trading partners.

China's leaders have two often contradictory interests. The first is communist ideology. The second is survival, which means not only physical survival but also economic growth and development. Under Deng Xiaoping and his pragmatic colleagues, survival is in the ascendant over ideology. We can help keep it that way by making sure China's faith in the West is constantly renewed and strengthened. If China loses confidence in our military power and our will to use it to deter Soviet aggression, it will have no choice but to seek a rapprochement with the Soviet Union. By the same token, if China's hopes for economic progress through increased trade with the West prove illusory, they will be tempted to turn toward the Soviet Union, despite their distrust and dislike of the Russians. An enlightened, hard-headed U.S. and Western policy to meet China's needs for both security and economic progress will assure that China is not faced with that Hobson's choice.

Too many people assume that the United States has the primary responsibility for satisfying China's need for economic progress. Our role is significant. But Western Europe's trade with China in 1982 was equal to ours, and Japan's was twice as much. Europe and Japan have as great a stake as we do in helping China develop its economic strength so that it will be able to build the necessary military power to deter Soviet aggression.

The Sino-Soviet split in 1961 and the U.S.-China rapprochement in 1972 were the most significant geopolitical events of the post-World War II era. The West has no higher priority than to pursue policies which will convince the Chinese leaders that their hopes for security and economic progress will be realized if they turn West rather than turning to the polar bear in the north. There can be no real peace in Asia if China comes under Soviet domination.

THE THIRD WORLD

The greatest threat to peace comes not from the possibility of a direct conflict between the United States and the Soviet Union, but from the chance that a small war in the Third World will drag in the two superpowers and escalate into a world war. If our goal is real peace, we must address ourselves to the conditions in the Third World that bring about conflict and war.

Three and a quarter billion people live in the developing nations of Africa, Latin America, the Middle East, and Asia, the vast majority of them in abject poverty. Their average per capita income is $600 a year, compared with $10,000 in the United States. Their societies are starkly divided between the very rich and the very poor. Their governments are seldom democratic and often corrupt.

Poverty and bad government are nothing new. What is new is that millions who endure poverty and bad government can now know what they are missing. To see how the other half lives all they have to do is switch on their television sets. Their realization that those who live in the West are far more wealthy, far more comfortable, and far better fed has created enormous frustration and tension throughout the developing world.

This tension and frustration make revolutionary change inevitable. The question is whether change will come by peaceful means or by violence, whether it destroys or builds, whether it will leave totalitarianism or freedom in its wake.

Although the Soviet Union is the source of many of the conflicts in the Third World and profits from most of them, it is not the only cause. If the Soviet Union did not exist there would still be regional conflicts and civil wars. The Palestinian people would still fight for a homeland, Iran and Iraq would still be at war, and India and Pakistan, two of the world's poorest countries, would still be spending $8 billion a year on defense—not because they fear the Soviets, but because they fear each other.

Still, even in these conflicts the Soviet Union is sometimes an instigator, sometimes a facilitator, occasionally an observer waiting for the right moment for taking an active role. In virtually every region of the world—the Middle East, the Persian Gulf, Southeast Asia, the Asian subcontinent, Latin America—the Soviets are involved in one way or another in doing what they do best: making bad situations worse. Their long-term goal is to initiate or assist in the overthrow of any government that is not under communist domination, especially in the Third World where regimes are often temptingly unstable.

The stakes are high, for it is not just the Third World that is at stake. When the interests of the great powers collide in areas like the Middle East and the Persian Gulf, any small war between their respective allies can rapidly escalate into a world war. In the Middle East crises of 1956, 1958, 1967, and 1973, for example, the superpowers were drawn toward the precipice of direct conflict by the actions of their allies in the region. The world saw how easily the cradle of civilization could become its grave.

The most immediate threat to peace in the Third World is Soviet adventurism—not overt aggression across borders by Soviet troops as in Afghanistan, but covert aggression under borders by Soviet proxy forces.

The Soviets are shrewd observers of the international scene who know what the geopolitical market will bear. They avoid promoting invasions across borders such as North Korea's invasion of South Korea. In that case communist aggression provided a clear rationale for response by a united West.

Since the West is moved to outrage in such matters of sharp black and white, the Soviets have learned to do much of their dirty work in gray areas. Theirs is a thoroughly modern technique of expansionism. They provide arms, training, and propaganda support to revolutionary forces within a country. Their recent victories—in Yemen, Ethiopia, Angola, and Nicaragua—have been sleights-of-hand, backdoor operations in which their involvement was hidden behind local forces or proxies.

Overt aggression across a border entails great risk and cost in terms of worsening relations with the West, as was the case following the Soviet invasion of Afghanistan. Aggression-by-proxy is a low-cost, low-risk enterprise that can therefore be carried out on a far vaster scale. An indication of the success of this tactic is that nine countries and 100 million people have come under Soviet domination since 1974. Until Afghanistan no Russian soldiers were lost in combat in the process of bringing these victories about. Such conquests cost only as much as the weapons do. And the risk to Soviet interests is minimal, because the West usually directs its response against the proxy forces, not the source.

The West has not yet found an effective way to combat indirect Soviet aggression, and our weakness in this regard is one of the Soviets' greatest strengths. Their policy is one of sheer, ruthless opportunism; the West, meanwhile, struggles to find ways to combat covert Soviet aggression that are in accordance with accepted rules of traditional warfare. As a result we have found ourselves outgunned and outmaneuvered time and time again in the Third World because we have been unwilling to do what is necessary to win.

It is not that we should "sink to their level" in combating the Soviets. It is simply that we should be just as aggressive in promoting our ideals and in assisting our friends in the Third World as the Soviets are in promoting and assisting theirs. At a time when the Soviet Union's entire strategy is based on using covert rather than overt tactics, for instance, it would be the height of stupidity for the United States to castrate our CIA.

Our first step in building real peace in the Third World should be to end our romance with left-wing revolution. The catharsis of violent revolution has been so common in this century that many have come to think of it as inevitable. If we are to play a productive role in the Third World, and if we are to stop playing into the Soviets' hands, we must stop assuming that violence is the only road to change that developing nations can take.

Revolutions can begin without outside support. But they cannot survive and prevail without weapons, logistical expertise, food, medical supplies, communications equipment, and training. These things must be provided from outside the country. The North Vietnamese could not have conquered the South without the support of the Soviet

Union. In Nicaragua the Sandinistas would have been hard-pressed to take power without the backing of the Soviets and the Cubans. And while there would have been a guerrilla insurrection in El Salvador without outside support, the guerrillas could not survive without the weapons they receive through Nicaragua, again from the Cubans and the Soviet bloc.

One nation falls after another, often with the help of communist leaders in nations that fell before. But eventually all roads and supply lines lead back to Moscow. In recent months shipments from the Soviet bloc have been intercepted en route to Central America. Crates marked "medical supplies" have been found to contain arms. Here in a nutshell is the essence of the Soviet policy in the Third World: the weapons of war wrapped in the empty promise of peace; the promise of soothing misery, the reality of exacerbating it.

We are a nation of idealists, yet we are often blind to the cynicism of Soviet foreign policy. The Russians make revolutions, and they feed on them. Like a vulture hunting fresh carcasses the Soviet Union scans the globe for potential troublespots, places where people are groping for a better way or suffering through periods of instability. Poverty and injustice do not produce communism; communism produces poverty and injustice. But the Soviets are skilled at exploiting peoples' grievances in order to bring about communist takeovers.

The Soviet challenge is total. Our response must be total. We must provide military and political support to governments threatened by Soviet-supported revolutionary forces. While this sometimes poses a difficult choice, it is rarely between a bad regime and a potentially good one. Rather it is usually a choice between an imperfect regime and a post-revolutionary regime that would be far worse.

The liberal critics cannot bring themselves to recognize this stark fact of international life. Time and again they have glorified and celebrated revolutionaries, no matter how inflated their promises or how vicious their tactics. And yet when have the critics been right? Do they believe now that Iranians are better off under Khomeini than the Shah, that Cubans are better off under Castro than under Batista, or that the Vietnamese are better off under the communists than under Thieu?

Still, simply opposing violent, communist revolutions is not enough. We must be able to convince people that they should fight against insurgents not just because of the fear of communism but also because of the promise of freedom. The people in these countries have terrible problems. The communists at least talk about the problems. Too often we talk only about the communists. It is not enough for us to point out that going down the communist road is the wrong way. The only effective answer is for us to offer a better way.

That is our task today in Central America.

In the 1970s the United States failed a critical test in Indochina. Central America, which has triggered the most bitter American foreign policy debate since Vietnam, is also the most important test of American fortitude since Vietnam. We have had nearly a decade to study the lessons of our past failure. If we fail again there will be no excuses and little hope that we will ever again be able to defend our interests beyond our borders.

El Salvador is only today's crisis. As long as Soviet ambitions remain there will be other ones like it. This newest instance of Soviet aggression on our doorstep, however, challenges us to find both an effective way to counteract a Soviet-backed insurrection already under way and also to stop future such insurrections before they are hatched. How we meet these challenges in the Third World will decide whether we will preserve Western civilization or preside over its demise.

Two things are at stake in El Salvador: American interests and the interests of the people of El Salvador. As far as resisting communist aggression is concerned, our interests are identical.

America's new isolationists are living in a dream world when they contend that what happens in "little" El Salvador does not threaten our interests. Apart from our concern that in the event of a communist takeover hundreds of thousands of refugees would flood into high-unemployment areas of Texas and other border states, the U.S. has a vital strategic interest in the outcome in El Salvador. Nuclear missiles based there would take only eight minutes to get to Washington. If the Panama Canal were blocked by hostile forces American shipping would be paralyzed. If the communists, who now have a foothold on our continent in Nicaragua, extend that foothold into El Salvador they will have a secure basing station for further forays—both to the south into South America, and to the north into Mexico and beyond.

The refrain of the new isolationists is unchanging and unending. In the 1960s, after Castro's revolution, they asked: "What can little Cuba do to hurt us?" Cuba became a proxy of the Soviet Union, a supplier of crack shock troops for conquests in Africa and elsewhere. One of its victims was Nicaragua, and after the Sandinistas took power there in 1979 the new isolationists were again in full chorus: "What can little Nicaragua do?" The Sandinistas, having made a mess of their own country by replacing a right-wing authoritarian regime with a left-wing totalitarian one, began to export *their* revolution. One of *their* targets is El Salvador. And just as they were not satisfied with Nicaragua the communists would not be satisfied with conquering the 2.4 million people of El Salvador. If the communists win there they will look elsewhere: Honduras, Costa Rica, Guatemala, Panama—and eventually the Soviets' big enchilada, Mexico.

Like many who were born and raised in southern California and the Southwest, I have great respect and affection for Mexico and its people. I went to school with Mexican-Americans for 16 years. Mrs. Nixon and I spent two weeks in Mexico in 1940 on our wedding trip. Our daughters' second language in college was Spanish. We have been back to Mexico many times for both public and private visits. As Vice President-elect in 1952 I attended the inauguration of President Adolfo Ruiz Cortines. He made a profound impression on me as being one of the free world's ablest and wisest statesmen.

Mexico's people are able, hard-working, and proud. But as a nation Mexico is dangerously unstable. It is a prime candidate for communist subversion. Over half a century of one-party government has left it awash in corruption. As a result of short-sighted economic policies and in spite of its position as a major oil-exporting country, its economy is in shambles. The strength of its currency has hit a record low. The Cubans, meanwhile, already have a beachhead in Mexico. The two countries have signed 27 major formal agreements on trade and other forms of cooperation. The Mexican far-left is fanatically pro-Castro.

We have learned over and over again that once they establish a beachhead, the communists always want more. Mexico and the other countries that follow El Salvador on the Kremlin's shopping list are the ones that have the most to fear both from the revolutionaries and from any hesitancy on our part about stopping them. For the moment the U.S. could endure a communist government in El

Salvador. To its neighbors such a development would be an immediate, mortal danger.

Resisting the communists is in the interests of all the nations of Central America. It is also in the interests of the people of El Salvador. There is no question but that El Salvador needed a revolution. Of the more than 80 countries I have visited I can think of none in which the gap between rich and poor was greater than in the El Salvador I visited in 1955. For generations the oligarchs had been squeezing the people dry. Reform on all levels of Salvadorean society was desperately needed.

In recent years, however, peaceful revolution has been under way in El Salvador. The current government, empowered as a result of a free, fair election in which 77 percent of the country's eligible voters participated, is working to bring justice and progress to a nation that has seen little of either. But it must also contend with a murderous insurrection by an 8,000-man guerrilla army, dominated by Marxist-Leninists and armed with Soviet-bloc weapons channelled through Nicaragua.

American media coverage is blatantly biased against the Salvadorean government. Virtually every day we hear or read of guerrillas and civilians being killed by government troops. The fact that in the past year alone the guerrillas have killed or wounded 7,000 government soldiers and murdered hundreds of innocent civilians receives only passing notice.

The senseless killing on both sides must stop. We should support efforts by the nations in the area to end the war by negotiation, but with two caveats.

We talk to bring peace. As we learned in Vietnam, the communists use talking as a screen for continued fighting.

Also, under no circumstances should we support the guerrillas' demand that they should hold high posts in a popular front government. A popular front would be a front for the guerrillas' ongoing revolution. Communists usually enter negotiations or coalition governments not to achieve peace but to achieve the same objective they had sought on the battlefield: total victory.

The choice is clear-cut. Should ballots or bullets determine what kind of government El Salvador will have? If the communists have so much faith in their system, why do they resist letting the people decide the question in a free, internationally supervised election? It is time to let the people of El Salvador decide whether they will have a better chance to get reform and economic progress under a Nicaraguan- or Cuban-style communist government, or under one supported and influenced by the United States.

Nicaragua is a tragic example of the kind of government El Salvador will get if the guerrillas win. When the Sandinistas took over many in Washington said we should just leave them alone. Keep the economic aid flowing, the revolutionaries' apologists assured us, and Nicaragua will flower into a functioning democracy.

Instead it is degenerating into a Castro-style dictatorship. A quarter-million refugees have fled the country. The villages of the Miskito Indians, who refused to be assimilated into the revolution, were burned to the ground. The free press was closed down, religious leaders were harassed, and citizens were taught to spy on each other Stalin-style through neighborhood "defense" committees. Children receive Marxist indoctrination in school. Meanwhile, real wages are down by 50 percent, unemployment is rising, and there are shortages of key foodstuffs.

With their people and their economy on the ropes, the Sandinistas turned away from problems at home to expansion abroad, building up a 138,000-man army, larger than the armed forces of all the other nations of the region put together, and prosecuting their "revolution without borders" in El Salvador and elsewhere—with the assistance of Soviets, Cubans, East Germans, and Libyans. As these foreigners flooded in thousands of Nicaraguans, including former Sandinistas, flooded out, vowing to return and oust those who betrayed their revolution.

In Nicaragua the U.S. policy of hands-off and handouts—including $120 million in aid to the Sandinistas from 1979 to 1981—didn't work. A policy designed to encourage the Sandinistas to allow more democracy only encouraged them in their belief that they could get away with less. A policy designed to leave them alone to mind their country's business only freed them to meddle with impunity in their neighbors' business. That is why the Reagan Administration began its covert support of anti-Sandinista rebels based in Honduras.

The Administration's Central America policies are designed to achieve three goals.

The purpose of our support of anti-Sandinista forces is to help the elected government of El Salvador by cutting off military supplies to the guerrillas. As British M.P. Julian Amery recently observed, "Experience has shown that a guerrilla movement can generally be beaten only if the base from which it operates is destabilized."

Our policy of economic and military aid to El Salvador is designed to strengthen the anti-communist government forces so that they can stop the communist-dominated revolutionaries, thus derailing Soviet hopes of subverting other governments in a strategically vital region.

A third goal is to quarantine Cuba and Nicaragua by preventing them from infecting their neighbors with their tyranny and their misery. In that connection the United States should not be defensive about our military presence in the area. We should not make threats as to what we *will* do. But even more important, we should not proclaim what we will *not* do. In attempting to reassure our own people we should not reassure our potential enemies. We should leave no doubt in their minds that we have the capability and the will to do what is necessary to stop the flow of arms from Cuba and Nicaragua into El Salvador.

The question now is whether Congress will support the President's policies or cut the authority and the funds he needs to continue them. In considering that question the critics should bear in mind that President Reagan did not create the crises in Nicaragua and El Salvador. He inherited them.

The specter of American men dying in Vietnam is being raised to defeat the Administration's military aid and training program. The comparison does not bear analysis. American troops were sent to South Vietnam because communist North Vietnam invaded South Vietnam. As the North Vietnamese have since admitted, they instigated, supplied and controlled the guerrillas in South Vietnam from the beginning. That was why President Kennedy sent the first American combat troops to Vietnam in 1962. Crack North Vietnamese regulars, not barefoot peasants, rode Soviet tanks triumphantly into Saigon in April 1975. Had there been no outside forces in South Vietnam, American troops would not have been needed.

There are as yet no outside troops in El Salvador. As long as this is the case no American combat troops will or should be sent there. Our policy in El Salvador and in other countries similarly threatened by revolutionary forces should be to provide arms and economic aid only. They must provide the men. If when adequately trained and armed they lack the will and the ability to defeat the revolutionary forces, we cannot do it for them. Even if we were to win, the victory would be temporary. As soon as we withdrew the revolutionaries would take over.

The doves who oppose military aid contend that the primary problem in El Salvador is poverty. Since poverty causes communist revolution, they assert, then we should deal with the cause by providing economic rather than military aid.

I first heard this argument in 1947, when President Truman asked the Congress to provide military and economic aid to Greece and Turkey. Thousands of postcards inundated our congressional offices. The message was simple: "Send food, not arms." Fortunately, a bipartisan majority resisted the pressure and supported the Truman Doctrine. If we had not done so and the U.S. had sent only food and not arms, Greece and Turkey would probably be communist today.

Both military and economic aid are essential. Either one without the other will fail to do the job. That is why the U.S. is sending El Salvador three dollars in economic and humanitarian aid for every dollar of military aid, a fact the critics persistently ignore.

The hawks contend that our primary emphasis should be on military aid rather than economic aid. This course would also be folly. Helping a government stop a violent revolution without helping it deal with the economic conditions that helped spawn the revolution would also buy only a short-lived victory. After one revolution was put down, another would take its place.

The critics—both hawks and doves—fail to recognize a fundamental truth about nations in the developing world: they cannot have progress without security, and they cannot have security without progress.

If there is one justifiable criticism of U.S. Latin American policy which applies to all Administrations since World War II, it is that we have consistently provided too much military aid and not enough economic aid for our friends and allies in the area.

But the worst mistake we could make in El Salvador or in any country under siege from Soviet-backed guerrillas would be to provide just enough military aid to keep them fighting, but not enough to win. If the Congress refuses to support President Reagan's policy with the funds he feels are necessary to prevent a communist victory, he will have no choice but to get out and let the communists take over. This would be tragic for the people of El Salvador and for us, but it would be worse to half try and to fail. We cannot afford another Bay of Pigs, where we sent a brave but pathetically undersupported force to be cut to pieces on the beaches of Cuba. And we cannot afford another Vietnam, where Congress was unwilling to follow through with the commitment we had made in the 1973 Paris peace agreements to provide the same amount of support to South Vietnam that the Soviet Union was providing for North Vietnam.

Such setbacks are bad enough for the people we let down. The legacy of our failure in Vietnam was over 100,000 boat people and three million Cambodians slaughtered by the communist Khmer Rouge government. But if it happens again the world may decide that failure is endemic to America, that our idealism and our good intentions, since they spell defeat for us and our friends time and time again, are burdens rather than blessings. Leaders everywhere will conclude, as did President Ayub Khan of Pakistan when he learned of U.S. complicity in the coup that led to the murder of President Diem of South Vietnam, "It is dangerous to be a friend of the United States; it pays to be neutral; and sometimes it helps to be an enemy."

The "how not to do it" pundits and congressional critics dominate the dialogue on Central America. What they fail to recognize is that while our current policy is not an ideal one, it is the least we can do under the circumstances. In the future, however, the United States should act *before* Soviet puppets such as the Sandinistas take power, *before* communist guerrillas can assail another freely-elected government such as El Salvador's.

To put it charitably, U.S. policy toward Latin America since World War II, while well-intentioned, has been inadequate, inept, and, worst of all, plagued by fitful starts and stops. Because of its proximity, Latin America should be our first foreign policy priority. But as I observed when I returned from Caracas in 1958, the only time Latin America receives front-page attention in the U.S. media is when "there is a revolution or a riot at a soccer game."

For decades the U.S. has been smothering Latin America with slogans. Foreign aid programs such as the Alliance for Progress and Good Neighbors raised high hopes in Latin America, and when the hopes were unfulfilled they raised hackles. Despite our good intentions we have broken our promises to the Latin Americans over and over again. Most of the billions of dollars we have sent to their governments have been sucked up by corrupt officials or wasted on poorly conceived or poorly managed projects.

Meanwhile we have left the impression that we become actively involved in Latin America only when *our* interests are threatened by communist aggression. We must now develop policies which also address *their* interests. Even if there were no communist threat millions of Latin Americans would justifiably demand reforms to lift the burdens of poverty, injustice, and corruption that have been their lot for generations. In addressing these concerns we will serve the interests of the people of Latin America and serve our own interests as well by depriving the communists of the issues they exploit to gain power and impose a new tyranny.

A top Carter Administration official recently said that after the flurry of high-level concern in the U.S. government as Somoza was falling to the Sandinistas in Nicaragua in 1979, Latin America was once again put on the back burner—until the crisis in El Salvador erupted.

It would be unfair to single out the Carter Administration for this tragic error. All postwar American Presidents, understandably busy with innumerable current crises far away, have not had the time or the inclination to focus on potential ones close to home. The tendency is understandable, but it must stop. We can no longer afford it. Since so many crises in Latin America and the other parts of the Third World are either instigated or encouraged by the Soviets, a modus operandi based solely on crisis management will give our adversary the advantage of always making the first move.

To stop the Soviets from reaping further grim victories, we must scan the globe just as they do. When all is quiet in the Third World, all is not necessarily well. The potential for unrest in a country often smolders just below the surface. Up until now we have only moved in to put out the fires of revolution once they start. In the future we must learn to keep them from igniting at all.

We need an early warning system for pinpointing these potential Third World hot spots. Once we identify them we must offer an active, workable alternative to communism.

Our goal is not to prove to people that our system is better than communism. They know that. Communism is something a country is infected with, not something it chooses. We must help those countries whose immune systems are low, build up those countries the Soviets and their proxies are apt to find most susceptible to their tactics. The West must learn how to practice preventive political medicine. More economic aid now could reduce the possibility that we would be called on for more military aid later.

The United States' responsibility in this effort should be principally, but not exclusively, our own backyard: Latin America, both Central America and South America. Since every Latin American country is a potential target for the communists, every country should be a target for us.

Our efforts, while directed primarily toward Latin America, should not be restricted to our hemisphere, and our allies' efforts should not be restricted to theirs. The Soviets' front lines in the fight for the Third World circle the globe. Their challenge is unified and centrally managed, and we will not meet it effectively if we simply divide the world into exclusive spheres of economic influence.

Soldiers wearing the uniforms of many NATO nations serve on the front lines in West Germany because each member of the alliance recognizes that what happens there affects its interests. We must grapple in the same way with the Soviet threat in the Third World. In the effort to strengthen the economic base of the developing world each alliance nation should act in the areas with which it is most familiar—the Europeans in Africa, for instance, and the Japanese in Asia. But each Western nation must also recognize that its interests are directly affected by events on the other side of the world, such as those in Central America. Likewise, European and Japanese efforts in Africa and Asia should not preclude the U.S. from assisting in these regions.

There is no reason why prosperity should necessarily exist north of the equator but not south of it. The West must find ways to teach what it knows. It will take an international effort involving both the public and private sectors; businessmen, government officials, educators, technical experts all must participate. If we are to protect what we have from our aggressive adversaries, we must share what we have with our less fortunate friends. Otherwise, it is through them that our adversaries may eventually get at us.

We need dramatic new initiatives to break the vicious cycle through which underdeveloped nations with authoritarian governments and some hope for the future are transformed into underdeveloped nations with totalitarian governments and no hope for the future. The West has been on the defensive for 35 years on all fronts—in Western Europe, in Asia and Southeast Asia, throughout the Third World. We must now go onto the offensive—not just in Central America but worldwide. We and our allies must be as bold and as generous in helping poor Third World countries get started on the road to economic progress as the U.S. was in helping Europe and Japan recover after World War II.

Obsessed with the idea that there is a limit to what we can do in the world, we have failed to press as hard as we could right up to that limit. In the Third World the Soviets exploit and extend human misery. It is our responsibility to confine and ease human misery. This is true of every nation of the Western alliance. The U.S. can show the way, however, by its actions in Latin America.

The threat of communist aggression is far more immediate to the nations of Latin America than it is to us. These nations' leaders are also far better acquainted with their peoples' problems and needs than we are. We should encourage and welcome their guidance and initiatives. They, in turn, should encourage and welcome ours.

Some Americans, believing we can duplicate our success in helping the nations of Western Europe rebuild after World War II, have called for a "Latin American Marshall Plan." The goal is excellent, but in pursuing it we must bear in mind that the Marshall Plan was officially called the European Recovery Program. In Latin America and the rest of the Third World the issue is not *recovering* but *getting started*. The Europeans were experienced in running sophisticated industrial economies. Most developing nations are not. Any economic aid program for Latin America will cost far more and take much more time to achieve results than was the case with our aid to Europe and Japan after World War II.

The debate over U.S. foreign aid is confined by two extremes. Some say we should cut government-to-government aid and increase private investment in Latin America. Others insist that more government-to-government aid rather than more private investment is the answer. In fact neither will work without the other.

Government-to-government aid should be used as fertilizer, to prepare the ground for private investment and thus for economic growth. Such aid is only worth the investment if growing conditions are right. If the government is repressive, the aid won't work. If the government is corrupt, the aid won't work. If the government has policies that penalize private investment, the aid won't work. If the government is so unstable that businessmen, workers, and consumers have no peace of mind, the aid won't work. Most important, since aid will not work without trade, we must expand the array of trade preferences we offer to our Latin American neighbors.

The Reagan Administration's Caribbean Basin Initiative is an excellent step toward achieving these goals. It should be substantially increased and extended to other nations in South America.

A massive increase in both *financial* aid and *human* aid—in which Canada, Europe, and Japan carry their fair share and the great bulk of which will be provided through private investment rather than government grants—is the best investment the West could make for peace, progress, and stability in the Third World.

While the Soviet promise is an empty one, we cannot beat it with nothing. We can beat it by recognizing and using the enormous economic advantage the West has over the Soviets. Our system works; theirs doesn't. Marxist economic policies produce poverty rather than progress. The only economic success stories since World War II have been written in the free countries of Europe, North America, and non-communist Asia. The Soviets can only brandish their power. We can give the gift of progress by helping poor countries up the first, most difficult steps of the ladder of economic development.

We can offer advice and even prescribe solutions to economic problems. But as far as political systems are concerned, we should be far more restrained and patient. While democracy works for the nations of the West, instant democracy is neither possible nor desirable for most of the Third World. We should hold fast to our ideals of human rights, but at the same time understand that a regime that provides some human rights is better than one that will provide none. The answer to those who contend that the U.S. loses in the court of world opinion because we support repressive anti-communist governments is that the most repressive governments in the world are communist ones.

The West has a long tradition of democratic government that most of the rest of the world does not share. But even the U.S., as prone as we are to hurling moralistic lightning bolts at regimes that do not come up to snuff on human rights, gave the vote to women only 63 years ago and guaranteed civil rights to blacks only 20 years ago. We must learn to be less harsh judges.

On the other hand, neither good moral sense nor good strategic sense compels us to subsidize an authoritarian regime's practice of repression. By its very nature such a regime will inhibit rather than stimulate economic growth, and without growth and stability a nation remains vulnerable to violent revolution—and therefore Soviet meddling. Just as we can deter Soviet misbehavior by establishing economic ties the Russians would be loath to give up, we can influence friendly but authoritarian regimes if we quietly but unmistakably let them know that our friendship will be even more profitable to them once they adopt less repressive policies.

If we give our friends nothing but public lectures on political morality, we create resentment and thus widen rather than narrow the gap between us. But if we give them economic support to help create stability and military support, in the form of aid and advice, against forces that threaten them with chaos, we will be sowing the seeds of democracy. Democracy is inevitably the first casualty of unrest and war. It is also an inevitable product of peace and prosperity.

To build real peace in the Third World, we must be patient with those who do not yet come up to our standards of political behavior. We must be loyal to those nations that choose not to threaten us. And we must be generous in sharing what our prosperity has given us.

In the countries where it has been established, Marxism has produced poverty, not progress; tyranny, not liberation; repression, not justice. Communism's performance has belied its promise. In the 1950s and 1960s, many leaders of nations emerging from colonialism understandably mistook Soviet successes in forced industrialization as the wave of the future. But the failure of socialism in the Soviet Union and in the Third World has been exposed in ways all can see. Eighteen countries in the world have communist governments. None came to power in a free election. And there is no country in the communist world whose leaders will risk having a free, democratic election. Today Marxism-Leninism is only a recipe small groups of ruthless men use to gain power and stay in power.

The Soviets have lost the ideological battle in the Third World. But this does not mean the West has won it. In the Third World, where change is inevitable, the West too often finds itself on the side of the status quo. If the choice is between the status quo and communism, the latter will prevail if only by virtue of the shrewd, cynical opportunism of the Soviet Union.

To win the ideological battle, the West must be opportunistic, too. It must aggressively seek opportunities to channel the energy of inevitable change in the Third World toward peaceful revolution rather than violent revolution. Today, the only kind of revolution on the market is too often the kind that the Soviets and their surrogates sell. Tomorrow, we can put them out of business.

PEACEFUL COMPETITION

In World War I, the slaughter in the trenches prompted many to call the conflict "the war to end war." Yet 20 years later world war again engulfed the globe, leaving unprecedented destruction in its wake and killing almost four times as many people. When World War II ended the nuclear age began, and the potential destruction of war increased exponentially. Today it is no longer an exaggeration to say that the next war would be "the war to end war" because it would also end civilization as we know it.

We must not court confrontation or flirt with war, but neither should we let ourselves be seduced by the idea of peace at any price. Mao Zedong elliptically expressed concern about this danger in my last meeting with him in 1976. He asked me, "Is peace your only goal?" I replied that our goal was peace, but a peace that was more than the absence of war. I told him, "It must be a peace with justice." If I had answered Mao's question with a discourse that emphasized only the need for peace and friendship, he would have considered me to be not only wrong but also a fool. After all, if peace really is our only goal, we can have it any time we wish simply by surrendering. The peace we seek must be coupled with justice.

To pursue peace with justice, the West must adapt its policies to the realities of the world today. Our policy must combine deterrence with detente. Detente without deterrence leads to appeasement, and deterrence without detente leads to unnecessary confrontation and saps the will of Western peoples to support the arms budgets deterrence requires. Together, they will lead to the containment of and peaceful competition with the Soviet Union.

Hard-headed detente requires us to concert our actions on several fronts. We must erect a shield of military power that will deter Soviet aggression at all levels. We need to make progress on arms control agreements that will reduce the burden of defense, reestablish the balance of power, and increase strategic stability in crises. We have to provide the Soviets with an economic stake in peace as a further incentive to stop their aggression. We must create a process for settling those differences between the superpowers that can be resolved and for preventing our irreconcilable disagreements from leading to war.

Peace and justice require nothing less of us. We do not oppose communism simply because our economic system is capitalist. We oppose its spread because of what it does to the people forced to live under its rule. Communism is an ideological bubonic plague. Wherever it has spread, it has made a nightmare out of the common man's dreams of a better life for himself and his family. It has broken up millions of families and has turned millions of others into refugees. It has killed tens of millions of innocent people and has enslaved nations. The first requirement of justice is that we block the further expansion of communism.

But containment is not enough. It would be wrong to hold a second Yalta conference, carving the world into spheres of domination and tacitly accepting the Brezhnev Doctrine that whatever is communist must remain so. It would be the height of injustice to purchase peace at the price of condemning forever to communism the millions behind the Iron Curtain. The Soviets will never accept the status quo in the West. We must never be satisfied with the status quo—East or West. We must never accept their rules for "peaceful" competition: that the Soviet bloc is a privileged sanctuary and that the West is their happy hunting ground.

The Soviets' goal is to dominate the world. They want to win, but without war. We also must try to win, but through peace. Our goal should be to engage them in a peaceful competition between our systems that will foster peaceful change in theirs.

Establishing a process for peaceful competition will require creative statesmanship of a high order. We must make the Kremlin leaders understand that aggression, direct and indirect, will lead to war. We must not object to their attempts to spread communism as long as they use peaceful means to do so. In one of our heated exchanges in Moscow in 1959, Nikita Khrushchev shouted, "Your grandchildren will live under communism." I replied that we had no objection to his *saying* this but that we would firmly resist if he tried to bring it about by force.

Regardless of the progress we make in reducing tensions that could lead to war, the United States and the Soviet Union are destined to continue to be all-out competitors. What the Soviets must understand is that, if the game is

to have any winners, they must abide by rules of engagement in areas short of war.

Our strategy for peaceful competition affects all of our
global relationships. We must unify the economic power
of the industrial democracies so that we can gain political
concessions from the Eastern bloc in exchange for our
economic cooperation. We must continue to develop con-
structive ties with China so that it chooses to align itself
with us rather than with the Soviets. We must seek to
alleviate poverty and repression in Third World countries
so that they do not become tempting targets for Soviet
adventurism. Above all, we must not stand aside and let
events control us. If we ride the hurricane, we will become
part of it.

Our most difficult problem in this competition is finding
a way to go over, under, and around the Iron Curtain to
carry it on in Eastern Europe and the Soviet Union itself.
We have no perfect solution, but this should not stop us
from applying partial ones. We must recognize that the
superiority of local Soviet military forces puts us at a
disadvantage in the short run but that the superiority of
our system and ideals gives us just as great an advantage
in the long run.

We must not treat the countries of Eastern Europe as
if they were part of a monolithic Soviet bloc. Those who
insist that we do so make the same argument as some did
when we opened the door to China in 1972. They say that
all these nations are communist, that communism is evil,
and that they are therefore all potential enemies and
should be treated as such. They fail to recognize the profound truth of British historian Paul Johnson's dictum:
"It is the essence of geopolitics to be able to distinguish
between different degrees of evil."

The extent of Soviet control, though great, is not total. The countries of Eastern Europe are allied with the Soviet Union in the Warsaw Pact, and East European communists and Soviet ones share the same ideology. The presence of Soviet military forces within and on the borders of these nations severely limits the scope of independent action their leaders can take domestically and internationally. But the governments of Eastern Europe have developed personal, national, and even some ideological differences. Some East European leaders have exploited these to eke out a small degree of maneuverability. This should not be overestimated, but we should encourage it through the bilateral relations we develop with each country.

The crisis in Poland exemplifies our dilemma. Our hearts tell us to give all-out support and encouragement to the Solidarity labor union and the anti-Russian and anti-communist sentiments of the vast majority of the Polish people. But our heads tell us that we cannot play a military role in Poland. We learned that lesson from the uprising in Hungary in 1956, when we appeared to offer support to the freedom fighters only to be proven helpless when the Red Army moved into Budapest. The Soviets will not permit an independent, hostile Polish government to take power, and they have the military power to prevent that outcome. We are left with the painful conclusion that it is better for Poland to be ruled by Polish communists than by Soviet communists, even though internally the two are usually indistinguishable by their actions.

This does not mean we are acquiescing to the Brezhnev Doctrine. The Soviets always assert that what is theirs is theirs and what is ours is negotiable. Unfortunately, the realities in Eastern Europe force us to accept the *fact* of Soviet hegemony, but we must never agree to the *principle* of it. We cannot set the liberation of the captive nations as our short-term policy goal, but we must never cease to proclaim it as our long-term goal.

Although Soviet power makes the cards in our hand seem weak, the magnetism of the West stacks the deck in our favor. How do we play out our hand? Their strong suit is in military power. Our strong suits are in economic power and in the power of ideas. If we play our cards wisely, the Soviets will be left holding theirs.

Increased trade and contacts can advance peaceful change within the Soviet bloc. There are those who argue that we should isolate these countries and let economic necessity force them to reform. They are wrong. The pull of a magnet is greatest nearby it. Similarly, the more contact we have with the East, the more we open it to the force of Western example. This will inevitably add to those internal forces that are generating change. During the long, chilly years of cold war confrontation there was little change in the countries of Eastern Europe. There has been substantial change since then. As I saw on a recent trip to four Eastern European countries, the stirrings of greater freedom are there—economic freedom in some, political or social freedoms in others. And conditions are ripe for further change.

The changes taking place in Hungary today prove the point. Situated on the frontier of the Soviet empire, Hungary is exposed to unjammed Austrian radio and television broadcasts and has become thoroughly infected with the tastes and ideas of the West. General-Secretary Kadar, whom Khrushchev appointed after crushing the uprising in Budapest in 1956, is a dedicated communist but also prides himself on being a patriotic Hungarian. His country languished until he implemented economic reforms during the years of detente. His production figures, while not high by Western standards, are now the envy of the Eastern bloc. Yet he faces a dilemma. Progress requires more freedom for enterprise; more freedom means less control for the state. He must constantly ask himself how much power he can afford to give up without endangering his rule, but for now the reforms continue. Isolating Hungary because of our differences with the Soviet Union would snuff out the prospects for more reform.

Our other strong suit is in the realm of ideas. A visitor to nineteenth-century Russia said that "one word of truth hurled into Russia is like a spark landing in a keg of powder." Today, the fact that the Soviet system lives on lies makes it extremely vulnerable to the truth. Truth can penetrate borders. Truth can travel on its own power, wherever people and ideas of East and West meet. Russia has heavy censorship, but its people are starved for the truth. Sending the West's message through every totalitarian barrier—whether by exchange of visitors, or books, or broadcasts—will give hope to millions behind those barriers and will gradually eat away at the foundations of the Soviet system just as seeping water can erode the foundation of a prison.

We should not shrink from the propaganda war, either within the Soviet empire or in the rest of the world. It is not enough to condemn the evil of communism. We must also proclaim the promise of freedom. We should strengthen Radio Free Europe and Radio Liberty and set up counterparts of them to compete directly with Soviet propaganda in those areas of the Third World that the Kremlin leaders have targeted for aggression. Even in peace, the war of ideas will continue. We must be sure it takes place on both sides of the Iron Curtain.

One great benefit of a summit meeting in Moscow would be that President Reagan would have the opportunity to address the Soviet people on television. Not only could he dispel his image in the Soviet press as a reckless war-monger, but he could also present our point of view as the free world's most effective spokesman. Some scoff at the thought that such a speech can accomplish anything. After all, the Kremlin leaders are hardly concerned by their Gallup rating. But I had the opportunity to address the Soviet people in 1959, 1972, and 1974, and if the level of official anxiety over these broadcasts was any measure of their power, it was not insignificant.

Khrushchev often challenged the West to competition with communism. We should accept that challenge and broaden it, bringing to bear the spiritual and cultural values that have distinguished Western civilization. Whether or not the Soviets choose to compete in these areas, *we* should compete with all the vigor at our command. The Soviets need contact with the West. They need our technology and our trade. They cannot keep out our radio broadcasts today and may not be able to keep out our satellite television broadcasts tomorrow. They cannot seal themselves off totally from the world. When they crack open the door to reach out for what they want, we should push through it as much truth as we can.

Winston Churchill once observed, "Russia fears our friendship more than our enmity." Churchill's insight showed a deep understanding of the Soviet leaders. They understand that one of the greatest dangers to the Soviet system is contact between their ideas and ours, their people and ours, their society and ours. This proximity invites unwelcome comparisons. It plants the seeds of discontent that will someday blossom into peaceful change. But if instead we isolate the East and reduce its contacts with us, we would be casting away one of our most effective weapons against the Kremlin leaders.

If peaceful change turns the attention of Soviet leaders toward their internal problems, real peace will have a chance to take hold in the world. It will at best take generations for such a resolution to come about. This is plainly unsatisfactory for a people as impatient as Americans, who are accustomed to solving their problems overnight. But history seldom accommodates the hurried. As with anything that is truly worth having, real peace will take time, effort, and above all patience.

In the meantime, there is no substitute for vigilance. We must restore without delay the military balance of power at the strategic, theater, and conventional levels.

We must also continue to build up our economic strength. Ironically, those who fault President Reagan's foreign policy but praise his domestic policy may one day look back and recognize that his greatest contribution in foreign policy *was* his economic policy. A democratic country with a weak economy will have a weak foreign policy. By wringing inflation out of the American economy, President Reagan has established a solid base for a sustained and long economic expansion. A strong American economy will strengthen the economies of our friends and allies abroad. It will enable him to win congressional approval for the defense and non-defense spending that is necessary to achieve our foreign policy goals. It will put him in a stronger position in negotiating East-West trade deals. It will help him fight off forces that advocate protectionism. And it will buoy the world economy and thereby strengthen the vulnerable states that are on the target list of the Kremlin leaders.

We must engage the Soviets in a process of peaceful competition. If they could sell communism in the marketplace of ideas, if they could make their system deliver on its promises, then they would deserve to win the global ideological struggle. But they cannot, and they never will. Thirty years ago, many saw communism as a way to progress, but now its performance has caught up with its promises. It is not enough that the Soviet Union has lost the battle of ideas. It is essential that the West launch an offensive to win it. If we succeed in winning this battle on both sides of the East-West divide, we will lay a firm foundation for building real peace in the years ahead.

Without one key ingredient, none of this is possible. Sir Robert Thompson, the great British strategist, once trenchantly described national strength as manpower plus applied resources *times* will. We have the manpower. We have the resources. But do we have the will to act as a great power with the vision to move the world toward real peace?

There is no question that if there is to be an arms race, we can win it. There is no question that if there is to be an economic race, we can win it. There is no question that if there is to be a contest for the "hearts and minds" of the world's people, we can win it. But there is a question whether we can win the contest we are actually engaged in today: a test of will and determination between ourselves and the most powerfully armed aggressive power the world has ever known.

Real peace requires that we resolve to use our strength in ways short of war. There is today a vast gray area between peace and war, and the struggle will be largely decided in that area. If we expect to win without war, or even expect not to lose without war, then we must engage our adversary within that area. We need not duplicate his methods, but we must counter them—even if that means behaving in ways other than we would choose in an ideal world.

National will involves far more than readiness to use military power, whether nuclear or conventional. It includes a readiness to allocate the resources necessary to maintain that power. It includes a clear view of where the dangers lie, and of what kinds of responses are necessary to meet those dangers. It includes also a basic, crystalline faith that the United States is on the right side in the struggle, and that what we represent in the world is worth defending.

If the Soviet leaders look westward and see an American leadership that eyes their moves in a measured way, that refuses to bow, that walks without faltering, that knows what it is doing, that is determined to do whatever has to be done in order to prevail, then those Soviet leaders will not be tempted to gamble all in high-stakes throws of the dice. They will make their cost-benefit analysis and postpone or abandon any aggression that will not be worth the effort or the risk.

As we look to the future, we should do so with confidence. I do not believe there will be a world war. I believe there can and will be progress in building more peaceful relations with the Soviet Union. I believe our geopolitical competition will continue. But if we muster the will, we need not be pessimistic about the outcome. As one generation succeeds another, we will begin to see the process of peaceful change take hold in the Eastern bloc as it is already doing to a small degree in Hungary and China. In that change lies the ultimate solution to the riddle of peace. We will win in the long run, and win without war.

But we must avoid soft-headed overconfidence. History tells us it is not enough to be on the right side. The pages of history are strewn with the wreckage of superior civilizations that were overrun by barbarians because they awoke too late to the threat, reacted too timidly in devising a strategy to meet it, and because they lacked the will to make the necessary sacrifices to win.

The history of the world is a narrative of man's struggle to become free and remain free. Freedom has not come cheaply, and keeping it is not easy. We hold a responsibility to the future unique to our time and place. Nothing that today's generation can leave for tomorrow's will mean more than the heritage of liberty.

No people have ever had a more exciting challenge. Yet the American people sometimes become deeply disillusioned about playing this role in the world. The loss in Vietnam was traumatically painful. The burden of building the defenses of the free world is great. The fact that countries to which we give billions of dollars in aid vote against us consistently in the United Nations is maddening.

Without the United States, there is no chance for peace and freedom to survive. Without the United States, the dawn of the twenty-first century would open a new age of barbarism on a global scale.

But we must assume this burden not just for others but for ourselves. We have a spiritual stake in not walking away from a great historical challenge. President de Gaulle wrote, "France is never her true self except when she is engaged in a great enterprise." This is true of individuals; it is true of nations; it is particularly true of Americans. Only by participating in a great enterprise can we be true to ourselves.

There could be no greater enterprise than to build a structure of real peace. The struggle to protect freedom and build real peace can raise the sights of Americans from the mundane to the transcendent, from the immediate to the enduring.

During a meeting with Brezhnev in the Crimea in 1974, I jotted down this note on a pad of paper: "Peace is like a delicate plant. It has to be constantly tended and nurtured if it is to survive; if we neglect it, it will wither and die." Peace has barely survived in the rocky soil of the twentieth century. The violence of two world wars and scores of smaller wars has nearly uprooted it time and again. It has managed to survive, but is far from safe. It is not a grim burden but an inspiring challenge to build and sustain real peace. Given the alternative of suicidal war, we must not fail.